Church Court

PRACTICE NOW FOR JUDGING THE
WORLD AND ANGELS LATER

Sharon Foster-Gautier

TRILOGY CHRISTIAN PUBLISHERS
Tustin, CA

Trilogy Christian Publishers
A Wholly Owned Subsidiary of Trinity Broadcasting Network
2442 Michelle Drive
Tustin, CA 92780

Church Court

Copyright © 2024 by Sharon Foster-Gautier

All Scripture quotations, unless otherwise noted, taken from THE HOLY BIBLE, NEW INTERNATIONAL VERSION®, NIV® Copyright © 1973, 1978, 1984, 2011 by Biblica, Inc.® Used by permission. All rights reserved worldwide.

Scripture quotations marked AMP are taken from the Amplified® Bible (AMP), Copyright © 2015 by The Lockman Foundation. Used by permission. www.Lockman.org.

Scripture quotations marked ESV are taken from the ESV® Bible (The Holy Bible, English Standard Version®), copyright © 2001 by Crossway Bibles, a publishing ministry of Good News Publishers. Used by permission. All rights reserved.

Scripture quotations marked EXB are taken from The Expanded Bible. Copyright ©2011 by Thomas Nelson. Used by permission. All rights reserved.

Scripture quotations marked GNT are taken from the Good News Translation® (Today's English Version, Second Edition). Copyright © 1982 American Bible Society. All rights reserved.

Scripture quotations marked MSG are taken from THE MESSAGE, copyright (c) 1993, 2002, 2018 by Eugene H. Peterson. Used by permission of NavPress. All rights reserved. Represented by Tyndale House Publishers, Inc.

All rights reserved, including the right to reproduce this book or portions thereof in any form whatsoever.

For information, address Trilogy Christian Publishing

Rights Department, 2442 Michelle Drive, Tustin, CA 92780.

Trilogy Christian Publishing/TBN and colophon are trademarks of Trinity Broadcasting Network.

For information about special discounts for bulk purchases, please contact Trilogy Christian Publishing.

Trilogy Disclaimer: The views and content expressed in this book are those of the author and may not necessarily reflect the views and doctrine of Trilogy Christian Publishing or the Trinity Broadcasting Network.

10 9 8 7 6 5 4 3 2 1

Library of Congress Cataloging-in-Publication Data is available.

ISBN 979-8-89041-119-8

ISBN (ebook) 979-8-89041-120-4

Dedication

This book is dedicated to my husband. Thank you for allowing me to share our scriptural trivial dispute resolution experiences with the Bride of Christ.

2nd Corinthians 1:3-4 MSG
All praise to the God and Father of our Master, Jesus the Messiah! Father of all mercy! *God of all healing counsel!* He comes alongside us when we go through hard times, and before you know it, he brings us alongside someone else who is going through hard times so that we can be there for that person just as God was there for us.

Disclaimer

This book was written to help Born -Again, Spirit-filled, Faith-Based Christians settle their trivial disputes quickly. We are not a law firm nor do we provide secular legal advice nor do we claim to be experts on the United States Court System. Our teaching and commentary is, for the most part, based on Scriptures from the Holy Bible.

Contents

Chapter One
Where Are the Church Courts? 1st Corinthians 6:1-11
1

Chapter Two
Three Easy Steps to Quickly Settle a Trivial Dispute
23

Chapter Three
Not a New Concept for God's People
51

Chapter Four
Take Off Those Filthy Spiritual Clothes
59

Chapter Five
Put On Your Royal Robe
79

Chapter Six
The Judges' Character, Mediating Process,
Renumeration, and the Law
95

Chapter Seven
Judging the World and Angels
117

Glossary
133

About the Author
136

CHAPTER ONE

Where Are the Church Courts?
1st Corinthians 6:1-10

Do you have a church court in your church? Is there anyone in your church wise enough that can settle the disputes of the Lord's people? 1st Corinthians 6:1-10 asks us this question: "If any of you has a dispute with another, do you dare to take it before the ungodly for judgment instead of before the Lord's people? Or do you not know that the Lord's people will judge the world? *And if you are to judge the world, are you not competent to judge trivial cases? Do you not know that we will judge angels?* How much more the things of this life! *Therefore, if you have disputes about such matters, do you ask for a ruling from those whose way of life is scorned in the church? I say this to shame you.* Is it possible that there is nobody among you wise enough to judge a dispute between believers? But instead, one brother takes another to court—and this in front of unbelievers! The very fact that you have lawsuits among you means you have been completely defeated already. Why not rather be wronged? Why not rather be cheated? Instead, you yourselves cheat and do wrong, and you do this to your brothers and sisters. *Or do you not know that wrongdoers will not inherit the kingdom of God?"* Inherit what? That's right! The Kingdom of God! What is that? Glad you asked. Yes, you, as a born-again child of God, you have an inheritance, the pleasure of living your life in the Kingdom of God here on the earth as described in Romans 14:17-18 MSG: "It's what God does with your life as he sets it right, puts it together, and completes it with joy. Your task is to single-mindedly serve Christ. Do that and you'll kill two birds with one stone: pleasing the God above you and proving your worth to the people around you." God's Kingdom is a spiritual realm, a place that is ruled by God and His Word of Life, Light, and Love, Jesus Christ. It is a place where God's will is being fulfilled on the earth, and wherever God's Kingdom is ruling on earth there will be visible signs, wonders, miracles, healings, and deliverance from evil, poverty, sickness, disease, and all sin. Once you have entered in and can clearly see what belongs to you as a child of God, then and only then, can you go about possessing your inheritance of Righteousness, Peace, and Joy in the Holy Ghost. It is an abundant life, where everything in your

CHURCH COURT

life becomes new and made right so that your peace and joy is returned to you in full. As a born-again child of God, heir of God and co-heir with Jesus Christ, this righteous, peaceful, joyful lifestyle is called "salvation." In the Greek, salvation means soteria/sozo, which means saved from the penalty of sin. It is your inheritance, and it belongs to you, right now! It does not matter what ails you; God sent His Word, Jesus, to heal you according to Psalms 107:20. *The spiritual new birth of being born again is the entrance door to God's Kingdom*, to a life like heaven on the earth as stated in Matthew 6:10. "Your kingdom come, your will be done on earth as it is in heaven." In the book of John 3:2-7, there was a guy who asked Jesus what this born-again business was all about. "He came to Jesus at night and said, 'Rabbi, we know that you are a teacher who has come from God. For no one could perform the signs you are doing if God were not with him.' Jesus replied, 'Very truly I tell you, no one can **SEE** the kingdom of God unless they are born again.' 'How can someone be born when they are old? Nicodemus asked. 'Surely, they cannot enter a second time into their mother's womb to be born!' Jesus answered, 'Very truly I tell you, no one can **ENTER** the kingdom of God unless they are born of water and the Spirit. Flesh gives birth to flesh, but the Spirit gives birth to spirit. You should not be surprised at my saying; you must be born again.'" Psalms 103:2-3 describes some of the benefits that are yours living in the Kingdom of God. "God forgives all your sins and heals all your diseases." In Hebrews 5:8, we see that Jesus, God's Word of Life, Light, and Agape Love became the source of eternal salvation (healing) to all who obey Him. In obedience to King Jesus, the goodness of God is revealed in your life, and you will become a testimony to a lost and dying world around you. In Proverbs 3:3-10, we get some instructions on how to **POSSESS** our inheritance, this plan of salvation in the Kingdom of God. "Let love and faithfulness never leave you; bind them around your neck, write them on the tablet of your heart. Then you will win favor and a good name in the sight of God and man. Trust in the LORD with all your heart and lean not on your own understanding; in all your ways submit to him, and he will make your paths straight. Do not be wise in your own eyes; fear the LORD and shun evil. This will bring health to your body and nourishment to your bones. Honor the LORD with your wealth, with the first fruits of all your crops; then your barns will be filled to overflowing, and your vats will brim over with new wine." This is the healthy and wealthy God kind of life, with no sorrow added to it. Read on, further down to verses 13-18: "Blessed are those who find wisdom, those who gain understanding, for she is more profitable than silver and yields better returns than gold. She is more precious than rubies; nothing you desire can compare with her. *Long life is in her right hand; in her left hand are riches and honor. Her ways are pleasant ways, and all her paths are peaceful.* She is a tree of life to those who take hold of her; those who hold her fast will be blessed." Proverbs 10:22 puts it this way: "The blessing of the Lord brings wealth, without painful toil for it." We are instructed in Matthew 6:33-34, as God's children and offspring, not to worry about anything, but to seek first the Kingdom of God and His righteousness and everything you need will be given to you. Seeking first the Kingdom of God and His righteousness means you have made a conscious decision to turn toward God and submit to His Word. You make a conscious decision not to continue holding onto anxiety, worry, fear, doubt and unbelief, sickness, disease, poverty, and hopelessness. You allow God's Word, Jesus, to be Lord of your thoughts, words, and deeds. Put simply in Colossians 1:27 MSG, "The mystery in a nutshell is just this: Christ is in you, so therefore you can look forward to sharing in God's glory. It's that simple." Colossians 1:21-23 MSG tells us that "all of us Christians are a case study of what He does. At one time you all had your backs turned to God, thinking rebellious thoughts of Him, giving Him trouble every chance you got. But now, by giving Himself completely at the Cross, dying for you, Christ brought you over to God's side and put your lives together, whole, and holy in His presence. You don't walk away from a gift like that! You stay grounded and steady in that bond of trust, constantly tuned in to the Message, careful not to be distracted or diverted. There is no other Message—just this one. Every creature under heaven gets this same Message. We look at this Son and see the God who cannot be seen. We look at this Son and see God's original purpose in everything created. For everything, absolutely everything, above and below, visible, and invisible, rank after rank after rank after rank after rank of angels—*everything* got started in Him and finds its purpose in him. He was there before any of it came into existence and holds it all together right up to this moment. And when it comes to the church, he organizes and holds it together, like a head does a body." Salvation is God's Spirit-filled plan of saving you and all humanity from the wages of sin and destruction. If God's Word of Life, Light, and Love is working in you, the believer, it will restore and make everything right in your life. It is a place of peace, love, and justice. Yes, everything becomes new and made right. In 1st Peter 2:24-25 MSG we have further instructions: "We are to die to sins and come alive unto righteousness and be healed. You are instructed to return to the Shepherd and Bishop of your soul." Romans 1:16-17 tells us that this righteous life God has for us is revealed in believing the Gospel of Jesus Christ. Sin is defined in the Bible (James 4:17) as knowing the right thing to do and not doing it. Romans 14:23 says everything that does not come from faith (believing in Jesus Christ) is sin. 1st John 3:4 states, "Everyone who sins breaks the law, in fact sin is lawlessness" In James 2:8 it states the "Royal Law" is to love your neighbor as you love yourself. 1st John 4:20-21 says, "If anyone says I love God yet hates his brother he is a liar. For anyone who does not love his brother whom he has seen, cannot love God whom he has not seen. And he has given us this command. Whoever loves God must also love his brother."

I found myself working hard at trying to obey this command of loving my brothers and sisters in the Lord when they were treating me badly. Quite frankly, I had not been in a very lovable mood toward my husband for a long, long time. I was busy trying to find out how to get justice! I had a trivial dispute with him that I did not know how to resolve. I knew how to get justice from a sinner who did me wrong. I would take them to the world's court system. But then I read in 1st Corinthians 6:1-10, I am not to do that to God's people who were treating me wrong. So, what was I to do? My experience at loving unlovable Christians was minimal, let alone loving a non-Christian who was offending me. Yet, those are the rules for living in the Kingdom of God and possessing this good life in Christ. According to Matthew 5:43-48 MSG, it says, "You're familiar with the old written law, 'Love your friend,' and its unwritten companion, 'Hate your enemy.' I'm challenging that. I'm telling you to love your enemies. Let them bring out the best in you, not the worst. When someone gives you a hard time, respond with the supple moves of prayer, for then you are working out of your true selves, your God-created selves. This is what God does. He gives his best—the sun to warm and the rain to nourish—to everyone, regardless: the good and bad, the nice and nasty. If all you do is love the lovable, do you expect a bonus? Anybody can do that. If you simply say hello to those who greet you, do you expect a medal? Any run-of-the-mill sinner does that. In a word, what I'm saying is, *Grow up*. You're kingdom subjects. Now live like it. Live out your God-created identity. Live generously and graciously toward others, the way God lives toward you." Gee! How could I say I love God who I can't see, if I couldn't love my Christian husband, who I could see. I was a work in progress!

I grew up in the country on a 100-acre farm in a Christian family of eleven siblings. As far back as I can remember, we were always in church. When I was very young, my father became the pastor of our church, and that is where I worshipped the Lord until I graduated from high school. My mom, being the pastor's wife, birthed twelve children. One was stillborn and the rest of us grew up together under the strict discipline of my father. Dispute resolution in my father's house, and there was plenty of it among the eleven of us, was a belt on the bottom. Proverbs 13:24 says whoever spares the rod hates their children, but the one who loves their children is careful to discipline them. We could not get away with disrespecting my mother or each other, or anyone else for that matter. As I look back, I must say I had great parents who loved the Lord and obeyed Him by loving us enough to discipline according to the plan of God. We did not learn a lot about the world's ways, as television was forbidden in our household. Whatever evils we did learn growing up, we mostly learned by being in the public school system. However, they were all quickly corrected with the belt while under my father's roof. Since all eleven of us were curious about what the world was doing, once we graduated from high school, most of us left the church and went with the ways of the world. 1st John 2:16 AMP says, "All that is in the world—the lust and sensual craving of the flesh and the lust and longing of the eyes and the boastful pride of life [pretentious confidence in one's resources or in the stability of earthly things]—these do not come from the Father but are from the world." After I graduated from high school and moved out of my parents' home, I don't think I went to church again until I was forty years old. For more than twenty-two years I went my own way, feeling free to make whatever choices I wanted on any given day. I went to community college, then transferred to and graduated from an Ivy League college. I partied, boozed it up, dated charming, ungodly men who mostly wanted to have sex but not get married. I opened my own modeling and social etiquette school. I even married a highly intelligent NY ungodly attorney who did not want anything to do with church, not even on Christmas or Easter. I thought I was going down the right road, making a good life for myself. However, I found myself empty, sad, and lonely. I had nice titles and lots of those nice material things that the world offered, but I was so empty, so sad, and so lonely on the inside. Although I was married, I did not feel loved. One day I found myself sitting at the kitchen table writing a letter to myself, I was asking myself why I was so sad. The loveless marriage to that ungodly NY attorney was not working. It had fallen apart from the beginning. I, on the other hand, was willing to keep it going at least until my son got out of high school and into college. The Ivy League degree was a great intellectual education, but I do not think I ever really got fully educated on how to love unlovable people. Growing up in my father's church, I knew I was supposed to do unto others as I wanted done to me. We were the preacher's kids, and most of the people in the church were nice to us. But how to love people who were not loveable, who were causing much distress, was beyond me. In those years of my conforming to the world's system, doing things my way and any old way instead of God's way, it was very painful, sad, and empty. I found that the extremely poor, all the way up to the extraordinarily rich people lied, cheated, stole, and fooled around on their spouses and relationships. I was very unhappy in that system. It seemed the more I conformed to those sinful ways, the colder my love for people grew. After my divorce from the attorney, I tried to date successful men, some Christians and some not. Since I was forty when I rededicated my life to the Lord, my dates were usually around the same age, and like myself, divorced. Many of them had been taken to the cleaners by bad divorces. They were packaged nicely on the outside, but on the inside, some were extremely angry and bitter. It was a frightening experience to say the least. One day I ran into a high school friend of mine who seemed to be peaceful and content. Come to find out, she was attending a non-denominational, Spirit-filled, faith-based church on a steady basis. She invited me to go to church with her. I resisted for a time, then relented and went. That is when I got born again and rededicated my life to Christ. I thought, *Finally, finally, finally everything is going to be all right!* For some reason I thought everyone in the church was mature Christians. I wanted them to be. I wanted to be in a safe place. I thought I was around a group of people who really loved each other and did things right according to the great salvation plan of God. Not so! I almost quit church for the mere reason that some of the behaviors of the church people were worse than my worldly ex-friends. There were a lot of people in the church in bad marriages, getting divorced, sick and unhappy, committing fornication, committing adultery, depressed, angry, and on lots of different drugs. Someone told me not to quit; they are in church for the same reason I was there, trying to get their lives lined up to God's salvation plan. Here I was, born again, in the Kingdom of God, and expecting this good, righteous, peaceful, joyful life in Christ. I thought it would show up automatically. It took me a while to learn that this God kind of life, free from sins, only came to me as I put my trust and faith and obedience in Jesus Christ, the Word of God. It tells us in Hebrews 10:38-39, "But my righteous one will live by faith. And I take no pleasure in the one who shrinks back. But we do not belong to those who shrink back and are destroyed, but to those who have faith and are saved." And Romans 1:17 MSG puts it this way: "It's news I'm most proud to proclaim, this extraordinary Message of God's powerful plan to rescue everyone who trusts Him, starting with Jews and then right on to everyone else! God's way of putting people right shows up in the acts of faith, confirming what Scripture has said all along: The person in right standing before God, by trusting him, really lives."

I was living, but not this designer, good life that God had prepared for me. Things were not right in my life; my peace was gone, and I was not joyful. I was having a horrible time trying to resolve my trivial dispute with my husband. It went on for years and years. I was not a happy camper. I needed help! Romans 10:14-17 MSG guides the Christian by saying: "But how can people call for help if they don't know who to trust? And how can they know who to trust if they haven't heard of *the One who can be trusted?* And how can they hear if nobody tells them? And how is anyone going to tell them unless someone is sent to do it? That's why Scripture exclaims, A sight to take your breath away! Grand processions of people telling all the good things of God!" But not everybody is ready for this, ready to see and hear and act. Isaiah asked what we all ask at one time or another: "Does anyone care, God? Is anyone listening and believing a word of it?" The point is: *Before you trust, you have to listen. But unless Christ's Word is preached, there's nothing to listen to."*

In Hebrews 11:1 MSG the Word of God tells us, "The fundamental fact of existence is that this trust in God, this faith, is the firm foundation under everything that makes life worth living. It's our handle on what we can't see." I had to learn to see me, my life, and others in the mirror of the Word of God exactly the way God sees me, my life, and others. He made me in His image and likeness and everything He made was very good! I had to start seeing myself and life through the eyes of God. A very good life designed by God, clearly stated in Genesis 1:26, 31. I needed to make some changes according to Ephesians 4:22-24: "You were taught, with regard to your former way of life, to put off your old self, which is being corrupted by its deceitful desires; to *be made new in the attitude of your minds; and to put on the new self, created to be like God* in true righteousness and holiness." The MSG version of Ephesians 4:17-32 makes the changes I needed to make a little clearer. "And so, I insist—and God backs me up on this—that there be no going along with the crowd, the empty-headed, mindless crowd. They've refused for so long to deal with God that they've lost touch not only with God but with reality itself. They can't think straight anymore. Feeling no pain, they let themselves go in sexual obsession, addicted to every sort of perversion. But that's no life for you. You learned Christ! My assumption is that you have paid careful attention to him, been well instructed in the truth precisely as we have it in Jesus. Since then, we do not have the excuse of ignorance, everything—and I do mean everything—connected with that old way of life has to go. It's rotten through and through. Get rid of it! *And then take on an entirely new way of life—a God-fashioned life, a life renewed from the inside and working itself into your conduct as God accurately reproduces his character in you.* What this adds up to, then, is this: no more lies, no more pretense. Tell your neighbor the truth. In Christ's body we're all connected to each other, after all. When you lie to others, you end up lying to yourself. Go ahead and be angry. You do well to be angry—but don't use your anger as fuel for revenge. And don't stay angry. Don't go to bed angry. Don't give the Devil that kind of foothold in your life. Did you use to make ends meet by stealing? Well, no more! Get an honest job so that you can help others who can't work. Watch the way you talk. Let nothing foul or dirty come out of your mouth. Say only what helps, each word a gift. Don't grieve God. Don't break his heart. His Holy Spirit, moving and breathing in you, is the most intimate part of your life, making you fit for himself. Don't take such a gift for granted. Make a clean break with all cutting, backbiting, profane talk. Be gentle with one another, sensitive. *Forgive one another as quickly and thoroughly as God in Christ forgave you.*" With the help of the sweet Holy Spirit, I soon learned to train myself to believe the truth of God's Word and to walk in love like my Father God. If I continued in the truth, it would set me free (it's called faith to faith and glory to glory). I needed to be rescued! I needed to resolve my trivial dispute. I was weary of it and was ready to take it to the world's court. On top of the marriage, I had another trivial dispute with my Christian tenants who moved into my rental and did not continue to pay rent. It is so disappointing when a Christian does you wrong. How was I to get justice? My husband said to take the renters to the world's court. But! I read in 1st Corinthians 6:1-10 that as a Christian, I should not be taking my trivial disputes with my brothers and sisters in the Lord to the world's courts. *So, I started looking for a church court. But where were the church courts?* No one had ever taught me about church courts. I never remember hearing a sermon on church courts. I did not know where to find a church court. So, there I was, living a miserable born-again life in the Kingdom of God, trying to figure out how to settle my trivial disputes with the tenants and with my born-again, church-going husband. God tells us that people who don't do the right thing will not inherit the Kingdom of God. We see that in 1st Corinthians 6:9-11 MSG. "Don't you realize that this is not the way to live? Unjust people who don't care about God will not be joining in his kingdom. Those who use and abuse each other, use and abuse sex, use and abuse the earth and everything in it, don't qualify as citizens in God's kingdom. A number of you know from experience what I'm talking about, for not so long ago you were on that list. Since then, you've been cleaned up and given a fresh start by Jesus, our Master, our Messiah, and by our God present in us, the Spirit." Yes, I had been given a fresh start by accepting Jesus as Lord and Savior and I wanted justice and my peace and joy back. How was I to get it with no church courts around to hear my case?

Look around you and tell me how many other church-going people are experiencing unjust practices from within the church fellowship. Are Christian families falling apart in divorce at the same rate as the world's? Is the stress and anxiety of the end times darkness causing broken families, sickness, disease, and oppression in the church of God at the same rate as the world? Does the sinner have more money than the King's Kids, the saints? Are we the city on a hill, the light shining in the darkness, the salt of the earth? *Do the Lord's people have church courts with a clear-cut plan of action to help God's people settle their trivial disputes?* If you were a sinner going to the world's court system and you wanted to resolve a trivial dispute, what steps would you take to file a lawsuit against the one who harmed you? As a Christian, going to the church court system if you wanted to resolve a trivial dispute, what steps would you take to file a lawsuit against the brother or sister in the Lord who harmed you? *Where is that church court?* What is the law that would be the basis for a church court ruling on trivial disputes among the brothers and sisters, the Lord's people? According to James 2:8, "If you really keep the Royal Law found in the scriptures, 'Love your neighbor as yourself' you are doing right." Romans 13:10 says, "Love does no harm to a neighbor; therefore, love is the fulfillment of the law."

How many Christians, like me, were assembling weekly, listening to Godly sermons but were not diligently and consistently practicing what we were learning? How many of the Lord's people are forsaking their inheritance of Righteousness, Peace, and Joy in the Holy Spirit? Mark 4:24 says the measure we hear the truth, study it, and practice it = is the measure of return we will get. How could I possess this lifestyle without doing that? I enrolled myself in our church's Bible school and decided to put this lifestyle to practice. I was determined not to let sins lord over my life anymore. I was sick of it! I wanted the God kind of life where things are right, peaceful, and joyful. Little by little, step by step, I began to change my thinking, my words, and my ways to line up with the plan and purposes of God.

According to 2nd Corinthians 8:7, *I should be excelling in everything*—"in faith, in speech, in knowledge, in complete earnestness and in the love we have kindled in you—see that you also excel in this grace of giving."

Remembering previous times when I was single and around forty years old, my pastor was preaching from the Word of God, no sex without being married. What! No sex without being legally married in the eyes of God? I thought to myself, *what's a girl supposed to do?* Then the preacher said as a Christian you are not supposed to worry about anything; instead, pray and ask God for what you want, ask according to His instruction in Philippians 4:4-end. So, I prayed and asked God for a Godly husband. The dating game was not working for me. Then again on another Sunday the preacher preached, "If you want a saved mate, come to the altar and we will pray and agree with you to get one." I went to the altar by faith in God's Word. In 1st Corinthians 7:8-9 MSG Paul writes, "Tell the unmarried and widows that singleness might well be the best thing for them, as it has been for me. But if they can't manage their desires and emotions, they should by all means go ahead and get married. The difficulties of marriage are preferable by far to a sexually tortured life as a single." They also told us to write out a list of everything we wanted in a mate before we asked God for them. That way we would recognize them when they came along. So, I wrote out my extensive list of qualifications for the perfect husband. Nothing happened for a while, then one evening as I was praying by my bedside, I amended my list. I said, "God, please give me a husband that is born again, saved, and loves You. If they love You, they will do what is right and I will not have to worry about the rest." I knew that scripture in John 14:15-31 GNT: "If you love me, you will obey my commandments," because shortly after I rededicated my life to Christ, something inside of me kept saying "If you love Me, you will obey Me, if you love Me, you will obey Me, if you love Me you will obey Me." I did not know what it meant at that time; however, as I was telling a devout Christian girl about it, she said, "That is God talking to you." I said, "God! Talking to me? The God of the universe? Talking to me?"

She said, "Yeah! If you love Him, you will obey Him."

I said, "Obey what?"

She said, "The Bible!"

I said I had never read the Bible front to back and I did not know what was in the Creator's Manual of Life. I only knew what the preachers were telling me. At any rate, through the course of time the Holy Spirit pointed out my husband to me. Shortly after that amended prayer, I was coming out of the pew one Sunday morning rushing to the back of the church to go to the bookstore to get the recorded message. As I was crossing the back of the church, I walked by someone sitting on the back pew. As I passed by, he said *Hello!* I did not pay too much attention as I wanted to get to the bookstore. I turned my head, said hello, and kept moving. All I saw was green eyes.

By the time I got to the doorway of the bookstore some six feet away from the back pew where he was sitting, the Holy Spirit said, "*That is your husband.*" I was shocked! I turned to see who he was. He was gone! I went home that day puzzled. How could the Holy Spirit say that to me, and the person was gone? I had no way of finding out who he was or how to contact him. It was an exceptionally long week. Since living in the world's system for all those years, all this business of obeying God and listening to the voice of Holy Spirit, I had to learn it all over again. I said to God, "How could You tell me that was my husband, and he is gone, and I don't know how to find him?"

The long story made short, the next Sunday as the service let out, there he was! As I got up to leave my pew, someone said *Hello!* I looked up and there were those green eyes again. Oh my! There he was, appearing just like that! As quickly as he had vanished last week, he reappeared. He invited me to go to an insurance meeting with him, and I gladly agreed. I would not let him out of my sight this time. I went to the meeting and halfway through I came to my senses and jumped up and ran home. I thought, *I don't know this guy.* But he pursued me! We were married within six months of meeting one another. How wonderful! Surely nothing could go wrong now since the Holy Spirit had pointed him out. Righteousness, peace, and joy in the Holy Spirit surely was to be mine! The preacher had given us marriage counseling before he wed us. We promised God and each other to do right to one another. After about a year of being married to my Godly, Christian, church-going, born-again husband, I was headed to the world's divorce courts again.

#3 GO TO CHURCH COURT

#2 GO BACK WITH 2-3 WITNESSES

#1 GO TO THE OFFENDER WITH YOUR SCRIPTURES

CHAPTER TWO

Three Easy Steps to Quickly Settle Your Trivial Disputes

My Godly man was doing a lot of things that were not Godly. Since at the time, I had no concept of growing up spiritually, I expected my Godly man to be perfect and a mature Christian. Well! Besides hopping to a new job every year or so, my Godly husband had roving eyes for other women. When I confronted him with these things, he ignored the job part and told me I was imagining things about his roving eyes. The problem with him getting a new job every year was that in the process of going from one job to the other, there was downtime. Downtime meant no money coming in between jobs, a probation period all over again with the new job, and never being able to plan a vacation or special holidays. I did know enough of God's plan from growing up in my father's household and church, that the husband should be providing for his household. I knew enough to know if you are married, your eyes should only be for your spouse. I kept trying to make him accountable and make the marriage work, but he would never admit he was in the wrong. Finally, I suggested we see a marriage counselor. I wanted the marriage to work. I just did not know what to do to make it work. He rejected that idea and kept trying to persuade me that I was imagining things and that he was not in the wrong about anything. With me threatening divorce, finally he consented, and we went to a marriage counselor. I needed this trivial dispute settled. I desperately needed help. If things were not working in the kingdom of God nor in the kingdoms of this world, what was I to do? We sat down to be counseled. The counselor asked us to bring up all the history of our past relationships. I was appalled! I thought, *I do not want to know all the sad things that happened in his past. I do not want to bring up all my failed relationships.* I vaguely remembered some scripture about forgetting the past. Philippians 3:13 AMP says, "Brothers and sisters, I do not consider that I have made it my own yet; but one thing I do: forgetting what lies behind and reaching forward to what lies ahead." (You are born-again, Spirit-filled Christians; if you never read your Bible, the Holy Spirit has nothing to bring to your remembrance. The Holy Spirit will lead and guide you according to the Word of God. I strongly suggest you read your Bible from front to back ASAP.) I wanted someone to hold him accountable for this "right now" trivial dispute that was happening in our household. I was at a loss of what to do. Do I go to the preacher and tell him my husband is not nourishing and cherishing me as the Lord cares for His Church, and that he is eyeing other women? How would I do that? How embarrassing that would be. We only just got married. How was I to go about getting this trivial dispute made right? Where do I get help?

We did not continue those worldly marriage counseling sessions. I had decided the best thing was to go to the secular court and get a divorce. But first, I wanted to talk to my mom, who had been married to my dad for over 50 years before he went to heaven. After his passing, my mom moved from our homestead in NJ back to her home state, Georgia. I headed her way for the holidays. Maybe she could give me some advice. Since she was still grieving the loss of my father, I did not get much help there. I left her house and headed to visit my oldest brother, the medical doctor who had been married to his lovely wife a long time. Perhaps he could give me some Godly marital counsel before I returned home to NJ. As I drove along, I was listening to my gospel tapes and music. I was thinking about how to go about getting this divorce in the secular courts. Then, out of nowhere, a thought came to me. "The thief comes **only** to steal and kill and destroy; I have come that they may have **LIFE** and have it to the full." (John

10:10) I was so taken aback with the thought, I slammed on the brakes and pulled over to the side of the road. The thief, the devil, comes **only to steal, kill, and destroy. I screamed aloud, "NO, you don't, devil!** You will not steal my marriage." I had prayed for a Godly husband. The Holy Spirit is the one that pointed out my husband to me. I realized what my problem was. I did not know what God had to say about marriage His way. How could I resolve a trivial marriage dispute where I had no idea what the guideline was? I realized I needed to get God's instructions on marriage and follow them.

When I returned to New Jersey, I asked the youth pastor to give me every book and scripture on marriage he could think of. I started to study what God had to say about marriage. Then I started praying Ephesians 5:21-33, "We submit to one another out of reverence for Christ. Wives, submit yourselves to your own husbands as you do to the Lord. For the husband is the head of the wife as Christ is the head of the church, his body, of which he is the Savior. Now as the church submits to Christ, so also wives should submit to their husbands in everything. Husbands, love your wives, just as Christ loved the church and gave himself up for her to make her holy, cleansing her by the washing with water through the word, and to present her to himself as a radiant church, without stain or wrinkle or any other blemish, but holy and blameless. In this same way, *husbands ought to love their wives as their own bodies. He*

CHURCH COURT

who loves his wife loves himself. After all, no one ever hated their own body, but they feed and care for their body, just as Christ does the church—for we are members of his body. 'For this reason, a man will leave his father and mother and be united to his wife, and the two will become one flesh.' This is a profound mystery—but I am talking about Christ and the church. However, each one of you also must love his wife as he loves himself, and the wife must respect her husband."

One morning as I was praying this very loudly, my husband was listening to my prayers. He told me he said to himself: *She's lying, I don't do that. I do not love her like Christ loved the church. I do not nourish her and cherish her. I do not wash her with the water of the Word of God.* He said the Holy Spirit corrected him and said to him, "That's what you're supposed to be doing." Now we were both aware of God's guidelines. We knew what we were supposed to be doing according to the salvation (healing) plan of God about our marriage. He could no longer inwardly deny the truth of God's Word and call himself a Christian. After that, I would constantly show these scriptures to my husband and remind him of what the Holy Spirit had said to him, but outwardly he was still in denial. Who was going to make him accountable? Again, I was in my prayer closet talking to the Lord. "Lord, do You see what is happening? How could You give me a husband like this? Lord, can't You see he is not obeying You?" While I was in prayer complaining about my trivial dispute, the

Holy Spirit said to me, "Sharon, get up and go love your husband the way I love you." I was stunned! I said, "It is not me that is wrong, Lord, it is him. Lord! I do not know how to love like that. I love people when they do everything right and when they do not, I do not want to be around them. I do not like them when they are not doing things that are right." The Holy Spirit said to me, "I loved you while you were a sinner. You did not have to get everything right for Me to love you."

I thought about that for a long time in my prayer closet. I thought about how miserable my life had gotten while I was doing my own thing out there in the world system. In my backslidden state I was lost, empty, and sad. I wanted true, faithful, steadfast, unfailing love. Now here was the God of the universe, even after I had turned my back on Him and His Word, even while I was making a mess of my life; even while I was lost and lonely, He opened His arms wide to me and invited me into His Kingdom of right living, peace and joy in the Holy Spirit, right where I was at. I thought, *that's right; the Lord did not wait for me to get everything right before He loved me. He accepted me back into His arms of love and comfort and safety in my brokenness.*

I got up out of my prayer closet and obeyed what the Lord told me. I made myself practice loving my husband, right where he was at in his spiritual growth. It was extremely difficult! I did not want to have anything to do with him and his ugly behavior. I went into the kitchen where he was and I said, "What would you like for breakfast?" That was a big challenge for me at that time. At that juncture, he had been sitting around the house in between jobs, doing nothing but getting on my nerves. I, on the other hand, was working a full-time job, paying the house bills, had a full time Bible college schedule, and was studying for the real-estate brokers exam. The last thing I wanted to do was fix him breakfast. I felt cheated and betrayed. I really did not want to be nice to him at all. But, when I thought again how the Lord loved me, even while I was a sinner, I made myself obey God. I submitted to Adonai my Lord, the Lordship of King Jesus, God's Word of Life. I demonstrated the love of God to him in thought, word, and deed. I fixed him a hearty breakfast. I was not going to accept or agree with his ugly, ungodly ways, though. He needed to repent, to change his thinking and ways to line up with the Word of God in Ephesians 5:21-33 and love me like Christ loves the Church. However, I decided to keep on being kind, rather than being bitter and angry. Being angry and bitter had already sent me to the hospital twice with excruciating stomach pains. Yes, we needed help, but where to get it?

In Galatians 6:7-10 it says, "Do not be deceived: God cannot be mocked. A man reaps what he sows. Whoever sows to please their flesh, from the flesh will reap destruction; whoever sows to please the Spirit, from the Spirit will reap eternal life. Let us not become weary in doing good, for at the proper time we will reap a harvest if we do not give up. Therefore, as we have opportunity, let us do good to all people, especially to those who belong to the family of believers." My job was to learn how to persevere and walk in the love of God while the change for good was taking place. I needed to be patient while we both practiced obeying God's Word.

James 1:2-8 tells us that when are going through a faith test, we are to let patience have its completed work. You are to stay with it until you get your answer. You must anchor your earnest hope (expectation) that your scriptural prayer request, the answer to your trivial dispute, will happen as you activate a corresponding plan of action.

I was getting a bit weary doing good, to say the least. The deeds of change, lining up with God's Word, coming from my husband were long overdue. Both forgiveness and repentance must have an active corresponding plan of action for healing the trivial dispute to manifest. Fruit takes time to grow! Never take forgiveness and repentance lightly; there is healing there for both parties. I needed to forgive him, and he needed to repent and change his thinking and ways. It is a good thing to **always** be quick to forgive and let it go once a person says they are sorry and has corresponding deeds of repentance. Do not be proud and think it is your right to hold onto offense. It is a tormenting spirit that is hurting you, not the offender. A broken spirit dries the bones, causing sickness and disease to be in you. It is healing to remove yourself totally from evil and give it **NO** time at all. No evil thoughts, no evil words, and no evil deeds. It is healing to concentrate and meditate on the scriptural answer to your prayers. Proverbs 4:20-24: "My son, pay attention to what I say; turn your ear to my words. do not let them out of your sight, keep them within your heart; for they are **Life** to those who find them and ***health to one's whole body.*** Above all else, guard your heart, for everything you do flows from it. Keep your mouth free of perversity; keep corrupt talk far from your lips." Don't leave yourself open to evil tormenting your thoughts day and night. Shut evil down as quickly as possible. Get it out of you as fast as you can. Proverbs 3:7-8, "Remove your foot from evil, it is health to your navel and marrow to your bones." Not that the offender necessarily deserves it, but as a child of God living in the Kingdom of God that is part of your inheritance, your peace and joy! I can guarantee you if you let evil thoughts continue lurking around in your head, your peace and joy will soon be gone. Forgive! Be the first to give up evil! It is healing for you. Have words and deeds of forgiveness. Don't say you forgive, yet your words and deeds remain hostile.

If you are the one that must do the repenting or changing your thoughts and ways to line up with God's, get yourself a corresponding plan of action from your church court and put that action plan to work immediately. Remember, the measure you hear and practice God's Word is the measure of peace, healing. and joy that is returned to you. (Mark 4:24-29, James 2:14) Faith without a corresponding action plan is dead and does not produce the desired result. Your thoughts and ways go together. James chapter one says if you are double minded about it, you get zero results. Do not deceive yourself by hearing God's Word and not doing it. James 2:24 says, "You see that a person is considered righteous by what they do and not by faith alone." Romans 10:17 *tells us faith in God comes by hearing what God has to say about your trivial dispute. Once you know that, you come into agreement with God and His Word by your thoughts, words, and deeds.* 2nd Corinthians 4:13 MSG, "We're not keeping this quiet, not on your life. Just like the psalmist who wrote, 'I believed it, so I said it,' we say what we believe."

As you *practice doing the Word of God* you will see your life transform into the visible image and likeness of the God kind of life. Hebrews 10:38, "'So do not throw away your confidence; it will be richly rewarded. You need to persevere so that *when you have done the will of God, you will receive what he has promised."* Among other reasons to settle your disputes as quickly as possible is so your prayers are not hindered. It reads in Mark 11:25, "And when you stand praying, *if you hold anything against anyone, forgive them, so that your Father in heaven may forgive you your sins."* And then again in James 5:16 it says, "Therefore, confess your sins to each other and pray for each other **so that you may be healed."** Don't add up any of the wrongs (1st Corinthians 13:5) and do not return evil for evil (Romans 12:21). Do not be overcome by evil but overcome evil with good. In Philippians 2:14-16, "Do everything without grumbling or arguing, so that you may become blameless and pure, children of God without fault in a warped and crooked generation. Then you will shine among them like stars in the sky *as you hold firmly to the Word of Life."*

Righteousness, peace, and joy in the Holly Spirit is your portion, child of God. Do not let the thief, the devil, rob you of your inheritance. John 15:10-12 reads, "As the Father has loved me, so have I loved you. Now remain in my love. If you keep my commands, you will remain in my love, just as I have kept my Father's commands and remain in his love. I have told you this so that my joy may be in you and that your joy may be complete. My command is this: Love each other as I have loved you, and so that whatever you ask in my name the Father will give you. This is my command: Love each other." How will you get your prayers answered, how will you get your healing, if you don't have deeds of forgiveness and repentance? Unforgiveness can cause a root of bitterness to set hold in your heart. That root can grow into fruit and can defile you and those around you if you don't get it out of you immediately. Confess your faults one to another as quickly as possible, so that you may be healed. Give evil "0" of your time! Zero time!

Many Christians are sick because of unforgiveness. We don't want to forfeit any of our inheritance. There is no peace or joy in sickness or unanswered prayers. As 1st Corinthians 6:8-9 says "you yourselves cheat and do wrong, and you do this to your brothers and sisters. *Or do you not know that wrongdoers will not inherit the kingdom of God.*" A kingdom is defined as the territory ruled by a king. God's Kingdom is spiritual and is ruled by King Jesus. When you accepted Jesus as your Lord and Savior you got born again, spiritually born of God's Spirit of Love and Life, and entered this Kingdom where everything is right, peaceful, and joyful. Follow Jesus, and all your paths will be pleasant and peaceful. You will have a long life; length of days and peace will be added to you as well as riches and honor. You must die to sins (unrighteous thoughts, words, and deeds) and you absolutely must become alive unto righteousness, believing the Gospel of Jesus Christ. Then your soul, which is your thoughts, your will, and your emotions will respond to what is right and you will be healed! (1st Peter 2:24-25) You can do this! It belongs to you. God said so! Deuteronomy 30:11-16, "Now what I am commanding you today is not too difficult for you or beyond your reach. It is not up in heaven, so that you have to ask, 'Who will ascend into heaven to get it and proclaim it to us so we may obey it?' Nor is it beyond the sea, so that you have to ask, 'Who will cross the sea to get it and proclaim it to us so we may obey it?' No, the word is very near you. See, I set before you today life and prosperity, death, and destruction. For I command you today to love the LORD your God, to walk in obedience to him, and to keep his commands, decrees, and laws; then you will live and increase, and the LORD your God will bless you in the land you are entering to possess." Romans 10:8-13 explains to us just how close our salvation is. "But what does it say? 'The word is near you; it is in your mouth and in your heart,' that is, the message concerning faith that we proclaim: If you declare with your mouth, 'Jesus is Lord,' and believe in your heart that God raised him from the dead, you will be saved. *For it is with your heart that you believe and are justified, and it is with your mouth that you profess your faith and are saved.* As Scripture says, 'Anyone who believes in him will never be put to shame.' For *there is no difference between Jew and Gentile*—the same Lord is Lord of all and richly blesses all who call on him, for, *'Everyone who calls on the name of the Lord will be saved.'"[1]

YOU! MUST CHOOSE Life, the Blessing, the good spoken Word of God for your life, choose to believe in Jesus, and to love your neighbor as yourself. Do not be ashamed when you run into trivial disputes of any kind, we all run into them as we grow up spiritually. Remember, as I was growing up in my father's house with ten siblings, we had plenty of trivial disputes. We got over them quickly and continued to love each other. It can be the same way spiritually if you allow it. Settle your trivial disputes quickly and keep on loving your brothers and sisters in the Lord. Apply your three-step trivial dispute resolution plan God has provided for you found in Matthew 18:15-17. Do it now! Forgive and repent, and if necessary, go to church court and get it quickly resolved! Then, get back up and keep on following Jesus. He has great plans for you.

The more you practice, the quicker you will learn to love like your Father God. Ephesians 5:1-2 MSG: "Watch what God does, and then you do it, like children who learn proper behavior from their parents. Mostly what God does is love you. Keep company with him and learn a life of love. Observe how Christ loved us. His love was not cautious but extravagant. He didn't love in order to get something from us but to give everything of Himself to us. Love like that." How many times has He, Father God, forgiven you? Well, you get the point. Matthew 18:21-22 says, "Then Peter came to Jesus and asked, 'Lord, how many times shall I forgive my brother or sister who sins against me? Up to seven times?' Jesus answered, 'I tell you, not seven times, but seventy-seven times.'"

The fruit of God's Spirit growing within you, the love, joy, peace, kindness, goodness, gentleness, patience, faithfulness, takes study, practice, practice, practice, and time to grow. The harvest of what you are after is in the specific seed of the incorruptible Word of God. Plant that incorruptible specific Word of God seed (Luke

8:11) into your good and honest heart, a heart that is not crowded with rocks of unforgiveness and offense and weeds of doubt and worry Mark 4:24 AMP: "Possessing your inheritance, all things in your life made right, your peace and your joy in the Holy Ghost, your salvation, living a life free from sins will manifest if you are willing to persevere and apply what you learn." Practice living a trivial dispute stress-free life. James 3:16 says, "For where you have envy and selfish ambition, there you find disorder and every evil practice. Those who do those things will not inherit the Kingdom of God."

Hope came alive in me when I ran across Matthew 18:15-17 in my Bible study time.

Matthew 18:15-17

Here was a plan of action I could practice and believe to solve my trivial marriage dispute.

"If your brother or sister sins, go and point out their fault, just between the two of you. If they listen to you, you have won them over. But if they will not listen, take one or two others along, so that 'every matter may be established by the testimony of two or three witnesses. If they still refuse to listen, tell it to the church; and if they refuse to listen even to the church, treat them as you would a pagan or a tax collector."

1. If your brother or sister sins against you, **Go!** and point out their fault, just between the two of you. If they listen to you, you have won them over. But if they will not listen,

2. **Take** one or two others along, so that "every matter may be established by the testimony of two or three witnesses." If they still refuse to listen,

3. **Tell** it to the church (church court). If they refuse to listen even to the church (church court), treat them as you would a pagan or a tax collector/ expel from the fellowship. Once you have done everything your church court has ruled, you should look to be reinstated into the fellowship. (Go to **CHURCHCOURT.ORG** for your pocket size trivial dispute resolution manual, church court filing forms, elders pocket manual to set up your church court, and your very own "Victory Over my Trivial Disputes" journals." Church Court Institute is also there to help you get started.

I showed this passage of scripture (Matthew 18:15-17) to my husband and said, "Let's practice this. Since I cannot seem to get you to admit where you are going wrong, I am going to get two or three witnesses and bring them back with me and try again to resolve this trivial dispute between us. I will have witnesses that will know I pointed out your fault to you scripturally where you are going wrong." 2nd Thessalonians 3:10 says, "If a man does not work, he should not eat" and in Matthew 5:28 it says, "Anyone who looks at a woman lustfully has already committed adultery with her in his heart." I said to my husband, "I also pointed you scripturally to the right thing that you should be doing according to Ephesians 5:23 AMP: 'For the husband is head of the wife, as Christ is head of the church, Himself being the Savior of the body. He was still in denial. I called my sister. Both she and her husband were serving the Lord. I explained the dispute resolution plan to her according to Matthew 18:15-17 and told her I needed them to be my witnesses as I went back to my husband with all my scriptures and tried again to resolve my trivial dispute. I told her, "You are only coming along to witness that I did try to resolve the matter with him scripturally. You do not have to have been there when the offense happened." I told her I was having some serious marital problems. My husband knew what he should be doing in our marriage; I showed it to him in the scriptures. James 4:17 ESV, "So whoever knows the right thing to do and fails to do it, for him it is sin." Yet, he had not repented and changed his ways. I told her I already did step one and pointed out his fault to him just between the two of us alone, and I did it scripturally. I told him what God said about working and taking care of his household and wife. I told him what God said about the other women matter. I told her, "He doesn't admit that he is in the wrong." It is important when you are going to go to the person who offended you and you are going to point out their fault between the two of you, make sure you have the Scriptures with you that they violated, and bring with you the Scripture that they should be doing. Keep in mind, we are working out our salvation/healing plan according to the Word of God. God's trivial dispute resolution plan is based on Scriptures. Pointing out people's fault between the two of you must be based on Scripture, not pie in the sky. You also need to let them know that you know, and they should also know scripturally the right thing they should be doing. The offender may not be scripturally aware of either, so be sure to point out both the offense and the answer to the offense using scripture pertaining to your specific dispute.

I said to my sister, "I have not been able to resolve this trivial dispute with him, so I am doing what the Bible says to do next. I need two to three Christian witnesses to go back with me as I try to resolve this dispute." My sister said to me, "We cannot be a witness for you" and gave me her reasons. Now what was I to do? There had to be a way to get my trivial dispute settled. My number three step, according to Matthew 18:15-17, was to take it to the church. The church where my husband and I had wed, went to Bible college, and got ordained as ministers; those pastors had gotten divorced. I could not go to them for church court; they did not have one. After that upset in that church, my husband and I looked around for a church to go to. Finally, we decided to start one in our living room. We applied to and were accepted under the umbrella of a worldwide ministry. We had gone to some of their pastor seminars. I assumed they had to have someone in that big church, like 1st Corinthians 6:1-10 said, that was wise enough scripturally that could resolve trivial disputes. I wrote them a letter and explained the situation. I pointed out my husband's scriptural shortcomings and built myself up really good. I sent the trivial dispute in the form like a formal court document. (Court as in a place where trivial disputes of Christians can be heard by official mediators and then settled.) I called it a "verified complaint." I listed the complainer (plaintiff) as myself and the person to defend himself as my husband. I listed it as a civil lawsuit. The law being used would be God's Royal Law of "Love your neighbor as yourself." I included a form for my husband to answer and defend himself scripturally. I explained to the big church we needed a church court to help us resolve this trivial dispute. They set up an appointment with us and ministered to us. They were official leaders in that big church. They pointed out scripturally to my husband the Word of God on working and told him women are not stupid; that they know when men are eyeing other women. My husband tried to deny it with the elders of that church, but they quickly put him in his place. They corrected me also, and said I should not think more highly of myself than I ought to but in accordance with my faith. They gave us a scriptural plan of action to follow and to report back to them when we had completed it. We were both willing to follow the scriptural plan provided.

Finally! My husband was scripturally accountable to someone. Since our ministry was under their umbrella, if my husband did not comply, if they followed Matthew 18:15-17, he would get expelled from the fellowship. He would be as tax collectors or pagans. Thankfully, that did not happen. As we practiced the scriptural plan of action given us, over the course of time our marriage started to transform into the salvation-healing plan of God's Word. Practice takes time if you want your faith to be complete and lack nothing. James 1:2-3 says, "Because you know that the testing of your faith (believing God's Word for the answer of your trivial dispute) produces perseverance/(patience). Let perseverance finish its work so that you may be mature and complete, not lacking anything." The perfected and completed will of God for your life is that you be healed, and all your trivial dispute resolved. Patience does not mean to sit back and do nothing. Patience means you do not get bent out of shape while you are practicing the plan of action that your church court gives you. Hebrews 10: 35-39 says, "So do not throw away your confidence; it will be richly rewarded. You need to persevere so that *when you have done the will of God, you will receive what he has promised.* For, in just a little while, he who is coming will come and will not delay. But my righteous one will live by faith. And I take no pleasure in the one who shrinks back. But we do not belong to those who shrink back and are destroyed, but to those who have faith and are saved."

Sometimes the repentance, changing, transformation plan of action part may take time. Over the course of time my husband started to love me like Christ loves the Church. ("After all, no one ever hated their own body, but they feed and care for their body.") He also changed his ways with lusting after other women. Our church court hearing happened a few years after we got married in March 1996. With much practice and perseverance and our willingness to submit to the Lordship of Adonai, King Jesus, God's Word of Life, our trivial dispute got resolved. We have a beautiful, peaceful, joyful, God-like marriage today. Occasionally we may slip up and get out of the love walk, but we are very, very quick to forgive and repent. Healing did not happen overnight, but it happened. The Word of God became flesh! As for the trivial dispute with the unpaid rent from the Christian tenant... Well, we just had to forgive them and move on, because at that time we only knew that we should not take a Christian to the world's secular court. We did not know anything about getting justice in the church court.

It will do you good if you begin right now, today, to practice your three-step trivial dispute resolution plan that God gave you. Let the healing begin today. Ask yourself why you want God to forgive you of your slip-ups and faults and you are not willing to forgive others. Matthew 18:23-35 gives us an example of this selfishness. "Therefore, the kingdom of heaven is like a king who wanted to settle accounts with his servants. As he began the settlement, a man who owed him ten thousand bags of gold was brought to him. Since he was not able to pay, the master ordered that he and his wife and his children and all that he had be sold to repay the debt. At this the servant fell on his knees before him. 'Be patient with me,' he begged, 'and I will pay back everything.' The servant's master took pity on him, canceled the debt, and let him go. But when that servant went out, he found one of his fellow servants who owed him a hundred silver coins. He grabbed him and began to choke him. 'Pay back what you owe me!' he demanded. His fellow servant fell to his knees and begged him, 'Be patient with me, and I will pay it back.' But he refused. Instead, he went off and had the man thrown into prison until he could pay the debt. When the other servants saw what had happened, they were outraged and went and told their master everything that had happened. Then the master called the servant in. 'You wicked servant,' he said, 'I canceled all that debt of yours because you begged me to. Shouldn't you have had mercy on your fellow servant just as I had on you?' In anger his master handed him over to the jailers to be tortured, until he should pay back all he owed. ***This is how my heavenly Father will treat each of you unless you forgive your brother or sister from your heart."***

Romans 12:1-2 states, "Therefore, I urge you, brothers and sisters, in view of God's mercy, to offer your bodies as a living sacrifice, holy and pleasing to God—this is your true and proper worship. Do not conform to the pattern of this world but be transformed by the renewing of your mind." Conform means to comply, to act in accord or harmony with a standard and to transform means you will change in character, into the likeness of your Father God. Your spirit man is already the exact image of God; now your thoughts and ways must become Godlike. If you do not have a home church, ask God where your pastor and home church are. He will show you where to go. Get rooted and planted and immediately involved serving the Lord in your congregation with your spiritual gift that God gave you. Learn how to pay your tithes (10% of your income for the preaching and teaching of the Gospel.) In Matthew 23:23 and Luke 11:42 Jesus referred to tithing, the 10%, as something that should not be neglected and the offerings can be any amount you personally choose over and above the tithe, used to meet the needs of the saints (2 Corinthians 9:1-end). The benefit to you is that God blesses you spiritually and financially. Don't be a God Robber! These funds belong to the Kingdom of God. Mark 12:17 and Luke 20:22-25 record that Jesus said to them, "Pay to Caesar the things that are Caesar's, and to God the things that are God's." Taxes are collected as a revenue-raising measure to fund a government. We are funding the government of the Kingdom of God with our gifts of tithes and offerings.

The spiritually wise overseeing elder's job is to watch over you as you grow up spiritually. We all make mistakes as we grow up and need help resolving our trivial disputes. Get the help you need. If your new or old church does not have a church court, suggest they establish one, and recommend this book to them. And yes, you really do need great spiritual parents, just like you need great natural parents. Find yourself a home church and get planted there so they can help you work out your plan of salvation so that you may possess your inheritance (sozo/healing) in every area of your life. You are living in God's Kingdom and there is no lack of any good thing there: righteousness, peace, and joy in the Holy Ghost belongs to you. God says in Luke 12:32 AMP, "Do not be afraid and anxious, little flock, for it *is your Father's good pleasure to give you the kingdom.*"

Staying focused.

Here are some suggestions to keep you on a steady course after you have received your ruling from your church court. Purchase your personal **Trivial Dispute Resolution Victory Journal** from CHURCHCOURT.org and keep it handy. You can use the information you log into your learning journal to send in your quarterly progress report.

1. Daily thank God for the scripture answer to your prayer listed on page 2 of your journal.
2. Daily read your devotions from your personal *Trivial Dispute Resolution Victory Journal* aloud.
3. Watch dispute resolution VICTORY TESTIMONIES on your local ChurchCourt TV program.
4. Be faithful in attending and serving in your worship services and paying your tithes and offerings.
5. Keep open communication with your church court by sending in your written quarterly progress reports. Your church court should be measuring your accountability and success and responding to your concerns. Open communication can be done by both parties by phone, text, email, in person, or snail mail.

Expel and Restore: As for the judges who are mediating in your church court, Matthew 18:17 says, "... and if they refuse to listen even to the church, treat them as you would a pagan or a tax collector." 1st Corinthians 5:7-12, "Purge out therefore the old leaven, that ye may be a new lump, as ye are unleavened. For even Christ our Passover is sacrificed for us: Therefore, let us keep the feast, not with old leaven, neither with the leaven of malice and wickedness; but with the unleavened bread of sincerity and truth. I wrote unto you in an epistle not to accompany fornicators: Yet not altogether with the fornicators of this world, or with the covetous, or extortioners, or with idolaters; for then must ye needs go out of the world. But now I have written unto you not to keep company, if any man that is called a brother be a fornicator, or covetous, or an idolator, or a railer, or a drunkard, or an extortioner; with such a one no, not to eat. *For what have I to do to judge them also that are without? do not ye judge them that are within? But them that are without God judged. Therefore, put away from among yourselves that wicked person.*" In that case a certified letter from the church court would be sent expelling them from the fellowship until they were able to comply with the church court orders given. Once compliance has taken place, there should be restoration. Church court officials should bi-annually reach out to the parties to see if they are ready to be restored. Matthew

18:12, "What do you think? If a man owns a hundred sheep, and one of them wanders away, will he not leave the ninety-nine on the hills and go to look for the one that wandered off?" Galatians 6:1 AMP states, "Brothers, if anyone is caught in any sin, you who are spiritual [that is, you who are responsive to the guidance of the Spirit] are to restore such a person in a spirit of gentleness [not with a sense of superiority or self-righteousness], keeping a watchful eye on yourself, so that you are not tempted as well." Once reinstated, the matter should be under the Blood and not be mentioned again. Deeds of repentance and forgiveness have taken place, and the Lord says in 1st John 1:9, "If we confess our sins, he is faithful and just and will forgive us our sins and *purify us from all unrighteousness*." God doesn't remember it, and neither should anyone else. The church court clerk should keep records of all the progress reports that are sent in quarterly. If someone did not complete their probation in a secular court ruling, there would be a penalty to pay. Accountability to the agape love walk is important to the maturity of the saints.

CHAPTER THREE

Not a New Concept For God's People

The Old Testament way of settling trivial disputes for God's people is revealed in Exodus 18:13-26. It reads, "The next day **Moses took his seat to serve as judge** for the people, and they stood around him from morning till evening. When his father-in-law saw all that Moses was doing for the people, he said, 'What is this you are doing for the people? **Why do you alone sit as judge,** while all these people stand around you from morning till evening?' Moses answered him, 'Because the people come to me to seek God's will. **Whenever they have a dispute, it is brought to me, and I decide between the parties and inform them of God's decrees and instructions.'** Moses' father-in-law replied, 'What you are doing is not good. You and these people who come to you will only wear yourselves out. The work is too heavy for you;

you cannot handle it alone. Listen now to me and I will give you some advice, and may God be with you. *You must be the people's representative before God and bring their disputes to him. Teach them his decrees and instructions and show them the way they are to live and how they are to behave. But select capable men from all the people—men who fear God, trustworthy men who hate dishonest gain—and appoint them as officials over thousands, hundreds, fifties, and tens; have them serve as judges for the people at all times, but have them bring every difficult case to you; the simple cases they can decide themselves. That will make your load lighter because they will share it with you. **If you do this and God so commands,*** you will be able to stand the strain, and all these people will go home satisfied.'" Moses listened to his father-in-law and did everything he said. He chose capable men from all Israel and made them leaders of the people, officials over thousands, hundreds, fifties, and tens. They always served as judges for the people, **at all times.** The difficult cases they brought to Moses, but the simple ones they decided themselves. Then again in Deuteronomy 1:8-18 *you will see the confirmation of appointed judges to hear the disputes between God's people.* Notice in verse 17 this is addressed **to Abraham, Isaac and Jacob and to their descendants after them**. In Galatians 3:29 it states, **"If you belong to Christ, then you are Abraham's seed, and heirs according to the promise. That would be** *us, the born-again believers in Jesus Christ.* See, I have given you this land. Go in and take possession of the land the LORD swore he would give to your fathers— to Abraham, Isaac and Jacob—and to their descendants after them. At that time, I said to you, 'You are too heavy a burden for me to carry alone. The LORD your God has increased your numbers so that today you are as numerous as the stars in the sky. May the LORD, the God of your ancestors, increase you a thousand times and bless you as he has promised! *But how can I bear your problems and your burdens and your disputes all by myself?* Choose some wise, understanding, and respected men from each of your tribes, and I will set them over you.' You answered me, 'What you propose to do is good.' So, *I took the leading men of your tribes, wise and respected men*, and appointed them to have authority over you—as commanders of thousands, of hundreds, of fifties and of tens and as tribal officials. *And I charged your judges at that time, 'Hear the disputes between your people and judge fairly, whether the case is between two Israelites or between an Israelite and a foreigner residing among you. Do not show partiality in judging; hear both small and great alike. Do not be afraid of anyone, for judgment belongs to God. Bring me any case too hard for you, and I will hear it.'* And at that time, I told you everything you were to do."

Yes! Without a doubt, according to 1st Corinthians

6:1-10, God's people in the New Testament also have disputes they need to settle. People in the church are all growing up spiritually at different stages. Someone must be able to help them settle their trivial disputes according to God's plan, so they can grow to maturity, as Christ is formed in each of them. **Where are the church courts to settle these trivial matters?** If we are going to judge the world and angels, surely we should have a court system set up in the churches to help God's people settle their trivial disputes. They need to be able to go to their homes in peace, joyfully.

Proverbs 17:22 says, "A cheerful heart is good medicine, but a crushed spirit dries up the bones." Dried up bones can cause all kinds of sickness and diseases. Shouldn't we expect the born-again Christian to be accountable and to practice the royal law of loving one another like Christ loves us? The secular courts have penalties for disobeying the laws of the land. Where is the accountability in the Body of Christ to God's command and law that is recorded in James 2:8, "If you really keep the **royal law** found in Scripture, 'Love your neighbor as yourself,' you are doing right" in the church? When trivial disputes arise, is there a simple, clear cut CHURCH COURT system that can help you through and come out the other side victoriously? Tell me! Tell me! How many Christians are walking around with

CHURCH COURT

bottled up anger and malice, slandering one another? How many of God's people are walking around bitter because their brother or sister in the Lord has offended them in one way or the other and they do not know how to get past it? How many Christians have walked away from the Lord, from their natural and spiritual family relationships, because they do not know how to resolve their trivial disputes? Can I go to a church court system like the secular world goes to court to settle their disputes? In Romans 13:10 and 1st Corinthians 13:4-8 we see that "Love does no harm to a neighbor. Therefore, love is the fulfillment of the law." We see it again in Romans 5:14, "For the entire law (the Ten Commandments) is fulfilled in keeping this one command: 'Love your neighbor as yourself.'" Ephesians 5:1-6 instructs God's people to "follow God's example, therefore, as dearly loved children and walk in the way of Agape love, just as Christ loved us and gave himself up for us as a fragrant offering and sacrifice to God. But among you there must not be even a hint of sexual immorality, or of any kind of impurity, or of greed, because these are improper for God's holy people. Nor should there be obscenity, foolish talk, or coarse joking, which are out of place, but rather thanksgiving. For of this you can be sure: *No immoral, impure, or greedy person—such a person is an idolater—has any inheritance in the Kingdom of Christ and of God.* Let no one deceive you with empty words, for because of such things God's wrath comes on those who are disobedient." You may be born again and in the Kingdom of God, but are you possessing your inheritance? Are your scriptural prayers being answered yes and amen? Are you experiencing the peace and joy you deserve as a child of God? In God's Kingdom, you have a failproof system for your faith to work. Galatians 5:6 tells us, "For in Christ Jesus the only thing that counts is faith expressing itself through love." 1st Corinthians 13:8, *"Love never fails."*

Perhaps if we had smoothly operating church courts set up and made available to God's people, our families would stay together and the healing lines would be shorter. Perhaps there would be less sickness and disease in the church due to the stress of unresolved disputes. Do you want justice? Take it to your church court! Do not let bitterness devour you from the inside out, causing sickness and disease and broken families. Do not let disobedience or unrepentance and unforgiveness rob you of your inheritance in the Kingdom of God. Resolve your trivial disputes as quickly as possible. Do not be like I was. I did not know how to settle my trivial marriage dispute. That trivial dispute seemed like a mighty big mountain at the time. At times, I wondered if I could go on. There is no peace or joy when you are stuck (God knows for how long) in an unresolved trivial dispute. But, with the help of the sweet Holy Spirit, I did have the willingness in me to obey the Word of God and continue to practice the love walk until I got the victory! PTL.

CHAPTER FOUR

Take Off Those Filthy Spiritual Clothes

Ephesians 4:17-22 and 25-31 says, "*So I tell you this, and insist on it in the Lord, that you must no longer live as the Gentiles do, in the futility of their thinking*. They are darkened in their understanding and separated from the life of God because of the ignorance that is in them due to the hardening of their hearts. Having lost all sensitivity, they have given themselves over to sensuality so as to indulge in every kind of impurity, and they are full of greed. That, however, is not the way of life you learned when you heard about Christ and were taught in him in accordance with the truth that is in Jesus. You were taught, regarding your former way of life, to put off your old self, which is being corrupted by its deceitful desires. *Therefore, each of you must put off* falsehood and speak truthfully to your neighbor, for we are all members of one body. 'In your anger do not sin': Do not let the sun go down while you are still angry, and do not give the devil a foothold. Anyone who has been stealing must steal no longer, but must work, doing something useful with their own hands, that they may have something to share with those in need. Do not let any unwholesome talk come out of your mouths, but only what is helpful for building others up according to their needs, that it may benefit those who listen. And do not grieve the Holy Spirit of God, with whom you were sealed for the day of redemption. Get rid of all bitterness, rage and anger, brawling, and slander, along with every form of malice." **_Take a good look and see what dirty spiritual clothes you need to take off._** The Holy Spirit will help you get rid of those dirty thoughts and ways you used to wear when you had a sin nature. Remember, when you got born again you became a new creation in Christ Jesus, the old sin nature is gone, all things have become new (1st Corinthians 5:17). God forgave you of all your sins and He does not remember them as far as the east is from the west. Now in Romans 12:1-2 God expects you to change your spiritual outfit and be transformed to His likeness by renewing your thinking. This new thinking that you are to clothe your mind with will allow you start to see yourself as God sees you. It lines up with God's salvation (healing) plan for you which says in Jeremiah 29:11 AMP, "'For I know the plans _and_ thoughts that I have for you,' says the LORD, *'plans for peace and well-being* and not for disaster, to give you a future and a hope.'" This new way of thinking will allow you to change your old ugly ways as well. This old and dirty mental wardrobe is known as the acts of the flesh, or ungodly thoughts, words, and deeds. You used to wear these dirty spiritual clothes when you had a sin nature. But now, since you have become the King's Kids, you need to think, speak, and act accordingly.

Galatians 5:19-21 points out the obvious deeds of the flesh. The deeds of the flesh and the Spirit of God are contrary and in conflict with one another. The flesh, the old way of thinking and doing things, whoops it up and does not want to obey God. That way of living can get you into big trouble as a Christian. Remember, you not only want to enter God's Kingdom and see what belongs to you as your inheritance, but you also want to possess it.... in the here and now. Titus 2:11-15 says, "For the grace of God has appeared that offers salvation to all people. It teaches us to **say 'No' to ungodliness and worldly passions, and to live self-controlled, upright and godly lives in this present age**, while we wait for the blessed hope—the appearing of the glory of our great God and Savior, Jesus Christ, who gave himself for us to redeem us from all wickedness and to purify for himself a people that are his very own, eager to do what is good. These, then, are the things you should teach. Encourage and rebuke with all authority. Do not let anyone despise you."

THE ACTS OF THE FLESH ARE
DIRTY SPIRITUAL CLOTHES

Sexual immorality: involves any type of sexual expression outside the boundaries of a biblically defined marriage relationship Matthew 19:4–5 says, "Haven't you read," he replied, "that at the beginning the Creator 'made them male and female,' and said, 'For this reason a man will leave his father and mother and be united to his wife, and the two will become one flesh'?"

Impurity: a struggle to rid the soul of sin or contaminated thoughts

Debauchery: behavior involving sex, drugs, alcohol, etc. that is considered immoral

Idolatry: the worship of someone or something other than God as though it were God.

Witchcraft: the practice of magic for evil purposes; the use of spells

Hatred: intense dislike or ill will

Discord: lack of agreement or harmony

Jealousy: hostility toward a rival or one believed to enjoy an advantage

Fits of rage: strong and uncontrolled anger

Selfish ambition: when your ambition becomes all about you.

Dissensions: disagreement that leads to arguments

Factions: small, organized dissenting groups within a larger one.

Envy: a feeling of resentful longing aroused by someone else's possessions, qualities, or good fortune

Drunkenness: being in a temporary state in which one's physical and mental faculties are impaired by an excess of alcohol; intoxicated

Orgies: wild parties characterized by excessive drinking, drugs, and indiscriminate sexual activity and the like

I warn you, as I did before, that those who live like this will not inherit the Kingdom of God.

You must make a personal choice to change or renew your thinking to obey God's Word of Life. Deuteronomy 30:19-20 says, ***"This da**y I call the heavens and the earth as witnesses against you that I have set before you life and death, blessings, and curses. **Now choose life,** so that you and your children may live and that you may love the LORD your God, **listen to his voice**, and hold fast to him. For the LORD is your life, and he will give you many years in the land he swore to give to your fathers, Abraham, Isaac, and Jacob." **See! It is up to you!** God will not make you do anything. He does tell you to choose the blessing, choose life. Choose to believe in Jesus, the Word of Life. You are the one who must make a daily choice to practice being a doer of God's Word. James 1:22-25 tells us, "Do not merely listen to the word, and so deceive yourselves. **Do what it says**. Anyone who listens to the word but does not do what it says is like someone who looks at his face in a mirror and, after looking at himself, goes away and immediately forgets what he looks like. But **whoever looks intently into the perfect law that gives freedom and continues in it—not forgetting what they have heard but doing it—they will be blessed in what they do."** Possessing your inheritance is your choice, not God's nor the devil's. **YOU get to choose!** God says that people are without excuse. Remember after I got born again and rededicated my life to God's salvation (healing) plan, I was still trying to date these good-looking, ungodly, sexy, wealthy men. However, when I heard the preacher preach no sex outside of marriage, **I had to choose** to line my thoughts and ways up with God's plan ...or not! I wondered what I was to do! Then I was taught, according to God's plan, how to go about getting a Godly mate. The preacher said, "If you want a Godly mate, ask God for one and He will give you the desires of your heart according to His Word." His Word in 1st

Corinthians 7:1-5 says, "Now for the matters you wrote about: It is good for a man not to have sexual relations with a woman (do not fornicate). But since sexual immorality is occurring, each man should have sexual relations with his own wife, and each woman with her own husband. The husband should fulfill his marital duty to his wife, and likewise the wife to her husband. The wife does not have authority over her own body but yields it to her husband. In the same way, the husband does not have authority over his own body but yields it to his wife. Do not deprive each other except perhaps by mutual consent and for a time, so that you may devote yourselves to prayer. Then come together again so that Satan will not tempt you because of your lack of self-control." Keep in mind we are sticking with Holy Scripture according to the Holy Bible and dealing with the born-again spirit of humans. Matthew 19:4 said, "'Haven't you read,' he replied, 'that at the beginning the Creator "made them male and female," and said, "For this reason a man will leave his father and mother and be united to his wife, and the two will become one flesh"? So, they are no longer two, but one flesh. Therefore, what God has joined together, let no one separate.'"

That is exactly what I did, and God honored my prayer request. I had to get myself off the fornication list, having sex without being married. There are some smooth, sweet talking, super fine men out there. After high school, for the twenty plus years that I was living and conforming to the world's system, sex just was a natural part of dating. Don't forget, when I rededicated my life to the Lord Jesus, I was a single divorcee at the age of forty. When that preacher preached no sex without being legally married, I needed to understand how to manage that according to God's salvation plan. I was taught how to pray and receive a Godly husband. One girl told me she and her boyfriend got married to each other by standing under a tree and saying "I do" to each other with no witness and without the Word of God involved. What God has put together let no one put apart. You need to agree to God's salvation (healing) plans for marriage and every other part of your life you want made right. Remember, in the Kingdom of God your destination is salvation, not wrath. 1st Thessalonians 5:9-10 says, "For God did not appoint us to suffer wrath but to receive salvation through our Lord Jesus Christ. He died for us so that, whether we are awake or asleep, we may live together with him." In Romans 1:18-32 we read, "The wrath of God is being revealed from heaven against all the godlessness and wickedness of people, who suppress the truth by their wickedness, since what may be known about God is plain to them, because God has made it plain to them. For since the creation of the world God's invisible qualities—his eternal power and divine nature—have been clearly seen, being understood from what has been made, so that people are without excuse. For although they knew God, they neither glorified him as God nor gave thanks to him, but their thinking became futile, and their foolish hearts were darkened. Although they claimed to be wise, they became fools and exchanged the glory of the immortal God for images made to look like a mortal human being and birds and animals and reptiles. Therefore, God gave them over in the sinful desires of their hearts to sexual impurity for the degrading of their bodies with one another. *They exchanged the truth about God for a lie and worshiped and served created things rather than the Creator—who is forever praised.* Amen. Because of this, God gave them over to shameful lusts. Even their women exchanged natural sexual relations for unnatural ones. In the same way the men also abandoned natural relations with women and were inflamed with lust for one another. Men committed shameful acts with other men and received in themselves the due penalty for their error. Furthermore, just as they did not think it worthwhile to retain the knowledge of God, so God gave them over to a depraved mind, so that they do what ought not to be done. They have become filled with every kind of wickedness, evil, greed and depravity. They are full of envy, murder, strife, deceit, and malice. They are gossips, slanderers, God-haters, insolent, arrogant and boastful; they invent ways of doing evil; they disobey their parents; they have no understanding, no fidelity, no love, no mercy. ***Although they know God's righteous decree that those who do such things deserve death, they not only continue to do these very things but also approve of those who practice them."***

You cannot be a born-again Christian, a disciple of the Lord Jesus Christ, living in the Kingdom of God, and make up your own plans for marriage, sex, or idol worship. The Holy Bible is the Lord God's salvation plan for morally right living for all humanity, Jews and Gentiles alike. Accepting Jesus, God's Word of Love and Life, to be Lord of your life and allowing the Holy Spirit to lead and guide you is the way you get righteousness, peace, and joy in the Holy Spirit to manifest in your life. It is how you receive your healing in every area of your life. Today, we as Christians are the spiritual Jews who are circumcised of the heart. We are worshipping the Most High God; there is only one way to Him according to John 4:16 and that is through believing in His Son, Jesus Christ. God is agape love and God is a Spirit, and His worshippers must worship in the Spirit and in *truth.* (John 4:24, 1st John 4:8) One girl told me God is love and He loves people, therefore I can love (have sexual relations) with women because I love them. Yes, God is love and yes, God Almighty loves people so much that He sent Jesus to the cross to die, be buried and be raised again, so they could be reconciled to Him and follow His grand plan. However, there is NO sin in God. There are no exceptions to the Master's salvation plan of what is morally right in His sight. All idol worship and sexual immorality of any kind is sin in the sight of God. It does not matter if it is fornication or adultery or who you are doing it with. It has already been told to us three time, those who go against God's plan cannot inherit the Kingdom of God. Do not expect the God kind of life (righteousness, peace, and joy in the Holy Spirit) unless you want to agree with **HIS** salvation plan. Disobedience will separate you from the Life of God. In Jesus, God's Word of Life, there is zero sin. Zero un-right thoughts, words, and deeds. You do not want to incur the wrath of God by living in error, especially when your destination in God's Kingdom is to possess your inheritance, salvation, healing, peace, and joy in the Holy Spirit. Of course, you can't do something you don't know. But once you have been taught right, you should live right.

I have talked to only a handful of homo/bi/transsexual people in my adult life and was curious how they became involved in such behavior. Every one of them I talked to personally about it told me someone had molested them as a child. That may not be everyone's case but how terrifying and horrible for those that were. It seems that the child was instilled with fear and told not to tell anyone, or the perpetrator would harm them in some way or another. One guy told me he was repeatedly raped in his home as a child by men and the perpetrator took him outside and took a knife, slit his pet cat's throat, and told the boy if he told anyone he would do the same to his family. For a child that must be a continual nightmare. The first time I even heard of this was when my secretary at the modeling and etiquette school told me her father was molesting her and the mother knew but would do nothing about it. Finally, the child went to the police and reported the father, who I believed, she said got arrested. Child molestation seems to be a big contributor to homo/bi/transsexual behavior. On behalf of the love of God, I pray every abused person would be healed in Jesus' Name. It seems some people have been so scared that they have accepted this as normal sexual behavior and perhaps because certain governments at particular times in history have said it is okay. However, in Psalms 1:1 KJV God tells us, "Blessed is the man that walketh not in the counsel of the ungodly, nor standeth in the way of sinners, nor sitteth in the seat of the scornful." What kind of counsel can an ungodly person tell you, Child of God, about a Godly life? None! Our job as a born-again child of God is to delight ourselves in the law of the LORD; and in His law do we meditate (think about) day and night so we can observe to do it! In the Kingdom of God, if you continually practice error of any kind after you have been taught better, it is clear, according to Scripture, you will not possess your inheritance, salvation, healing, and peace. I overheard one non-Christian teenager trying to explain homo/bi/transsexuality to a younger non-Christian child who was not yet in their teens. In so many words, in her mind, it was legal because the government said so. No one had yet taught them God's salvation plan in Christ Jesus. If you are a born-again Christian and you choose to continue to live your life conformed to the world's ways, God will let you have at it! He said if you choose not to think it worthwhile to retain the knowledge of God, God will give you over to a depraved (the state of being corrupt, evil, or perverted) mind so that you do what ought not to be done. That sounds to me like you have been taught the ways of Christ, but you choose not to do them. People who are not born-again Christians, or who were and wandered away, like I did for about 20 years after high school, obviously live their lives outside of Gods' salvation (healing) plan. They do not follow Jesus, nor accept Him as their personal Lord and Savior. They make up their own plans and live their lives accordingly.

Without Jesus I had no hope, as I sat at that kitchen table writing a letter asking myself why I was so sad. I am soooooo glad I am born again, have entered the Kingdom of God, can see, and possess my inheritance of salvation. 1st Peter 12:2 says, "Like newborn babies, crave pure spiritual milk, so that by it you may grow up in your salvation." Hebrews 5:11-14 tells us, "I have a lot more to say about this, but it is hard to get it across to you since you've picked up this bad habit of not listening. By this time, you ought to be teachers yourselves, yet here I find you need someone to sit down with you and go over the basics on God again, starting from square one—baby's milk, when you should have been on solid food long ago! *Milk is for beginners, inexperienced in God's ways; solid food is for the mature, who have some practice in telling right from wrong.*" Let's repeat what Mark 4:23-25 AMP says, "'If anyone has ears to hear, let him hear and heed My words.' Then He said to them, '*Pay attention to what you hear. By your own standard of measurement [that is, to the extent that you study spiritual truth and apply godly wisdom] it will be measured to you [and you will be given even greater ability to respond]—and more will be given to you besides. For whoever has [a teachable heart], to him more [understanding] will be given;* and whoever does not have [a yearning for truth], even what he has will be taken away from him.'" **Access** to the Kingdom of God is available for all and is amazingly easy to enter. You open your mouth and pray aloud with honest intent and say, "Father God, I ask You to forgive me of all my sins. Forgive me for rejecting Jesus. I accept King Jesus as my Lord and Savior. Jesus, come into my heart right now and be my Lord and Savior. I believe God raised *Jesus from the dead.*" I think Romans 10:6-13, 17 is worth repeating. It says, "But the righteousness that is by faith says: 'Do not say in your heart, "Who will ascend into heaven?" (that is, to bring Christ down) or "Who will descend into the deep?"] (that is, to bring Christ up from the dead). But what does it say? *'The word is near you; it is in your mouth and in your heart,' that is, the message concerning faith that we proclaim: If you declare with your mouth, "Jesus is Lord," and believe in your heart that God raised him from the dead, you will be saved.* For it is with your heart that you believe and are justified, and it is with your mouth that you profess your faith and are saved. As Scripture says, 'Anyone who believes in him will never be put to shame.' For there is no difference between Jew and Gentile—the same Lord is Lord of all and richly blesses all who call on him, for, 'Everyone who calls on the name of the Lord will be saved." And in (verse 17), "Consequently, faith comes from hearing the message, and the message is heard through the word about Christ." Now that you are born again and have entered the Kingdom of God, you need to be to be baptized with the Holy Spirit. Acts 2:38, Acts 8:14-17 and Luke 11:13 share with you how to receive the Holy Spirit. Amazingly, at the new birth, Jesus comes right in and removes your old sin nature. You are spiritually birthed of the Spirit of God. You become a child of the Most High God.

As you grow up spiritually, no doubt, you will run into trivial disputes. Be quick to practice your three-step resolution plan.

Some time ago, a very wealthy Jewish acquaintance of mine told me he had all the money, buildings, and all the things that wealth could buy, that anyone could want. But! He said he had no peace! I said, "Oh! I know the Prince of Peace. His name is Jesus. Would you like to have the Prince of Peace come into your heart?"

"Yes!" he said, and he prayed that prayer aloud. Jesus came into his heart and the Righteous Spirit of God was birthed in him. All his sins were washed away at that moment. He was free like a bird, like a newborn baby with no history of sin. You could see the change in his eyes and his countenance. He walked around for weeks on a spiritual high. He said to me one day, "Can I say that prayer again?"

I said, "You do not have to say it again. Jesus came into your heart when you prayed that prayer. You are a new creation in Christ. You are born again, born of the righteous Spirit of God. What you must do now is to renew your thinking and learn the ways of Christ. You must learn how to follow Jesus. You choose to make Jesus, the Word of God, the Lord of your thoughts, words, and deeds. Make Him Lord of your life. You do that by finding a good Christian Spirit-filled church that teaches the whole salvation plan of God. When you read your Holy Bible, read it from front to back. Read it aloud. That is God talking to you and He will constantly be telling you about how much He loves you. When you learn to pray scriptures, you will be praying in line with His plans for you. Just so happens, the more you go to church and keep hearing about God's love for you and how He wants you to learn to love others and treat them the way you want to be treated, the more your personal intimate relationship with the Lord will grow. Everything will begin to go right. You will start transforming into the likeness of the One who created you. You will find peace and joy again as your thoughts, words, and deeds correspond with the master salvation (healing) plan. The closer personal relationship you have with your Creator, the greater the Peace of God will be revealed and manifested in your life. You can say that (Entrance) prayer anywhere at any time, day, or night. Just mean it with all your heart when you pray. Then immediately, find yourself a Spirit-filled church that has a church court, which will help you resolve your trivial disputes as you grow and transform into the image and likeness of the one who created you. Stay steadfast, faithful, and loyal and you will see the goodness of God show up in your life. Soon you will be mature enough to turn around and help someone around you that is lost and hurting. James 1:19-25 says, 'My dear brothers and sisters, take note of this: Everyone should be quick to listen, slow to speak and slow to become angry, because human anger does not produce the righteousness that God desires. Therefore, get rid of all moral filth and the evil that is so prevalent and humbly accept the word planted in you, which can save you. Do not merely listen to the word, and so deceive yourselves. Do what it says. Anyone who listens to the word but does not do what it says is like someone who looks at his face in a mirror and, after looking at himself, goes away and immediately forgets what he looks like. But whoever looks intently into the perfect law that gives freedom and continues in it—not forgetting what they have heard but doing it—they will be blessed in what they do.'"

Take off those dirty spiritual clothes of immoral thoughts, words, and deeds. Could it be that you are a citizen of the Kingdom of God, a child of the King, but not partaking of what rightfully belongs to you by exercising your saving faith in each of your trivial disputes? Sin and demonic evil spirits can weigh you down, bringing on the spirit of heaviness which can manifest in negative emotions, such as sadness, anxiety, fear, anger, or hopelessness. It can also affect our physical health, causing fatigue, insomnia, pain, or sickness. The spirit of heaviness is not from God, but from the enemy, the devil, who wants to steal, kill, and destroy your joy and peace. However, keep in mind Jesus has already defeated the enemy by His death burial and resurrection. Therefore, we can resist the devil and his schemes of deception by the Word of God and the power of the Holy Spirit, who lives in us as believers. You have a spiritual garment called praise you can put on to get rid of the spirit of heaviness. Praise is a powerful weapon, because it magnifies God and His attributes, rather than our problems and circumstances. If you need a evil spirit of addiction of any kind cast out of you, your church court can help you with that as well.

CHAPTER FIVE

Put On Your Royal Robe

"I delight greatly in the LORD; my soul rejoices in my God. For he has *clothed me with garments of salvation and arrayed me in a robe of his righteousness,* as a bridegroom adorns his head like a priest, and as a bride adorns herself with her jewels." Isaiah 61:10 AMP, and verse 3 says, "To grant to those who mourn in Zion the following: To give them a turban instead of dust [on their heads, a sign of mourning], the oil of joy instead of mourning, *the garment [expressive] of praise* instead of a disheartened spirit. So, they will be called the trees of righteousness [strong and magnificent, distinguished for integrity, justice, and right standing with God], The planting of the LORD, that He may be glorified." We are to "follow God's example, therefore, as dearly loved children and walk in the way of love, just as Christ loved us and gave himself up for us as a fragrant offering and sacrifice to God." Ephesians 5:1-2. says, "As the life of God's Spirit and character develops in you, the fruit of His love, joy, peace, patience, kindness, goodness, faithfulness, gentleness, and self-control will all start to manifest in your life; against such things there is no law. Those who belong to Christ Jesus have crucified the flesh (the secular worlds way of thinking and doing things) with its passions and desires. Since we live by the Spirit, let us keep in step with the Spirit. Let us not become conceited, provoking and envying each other." It is only right that everything in God's House, which you are, be a peaceful and a joyful place to live. "This means that anyone who belongs to Christ has become a new person. *The old life is gone; a new life has begun!*" (2nd Corinthians 5:17). **Come on, you are the King's Kids. Put on your royal spiritual clothes;** your garments of salvation (healing), and be arrayed in your robe of His righteousness (life in Christ made right). Resolve your trivial disputes quickly. May God Almighty be glorified! Start seeing yourself the way God sees you. Royal! Happy, healthy, wealthy, full of joy and full of peace! 3rd John 1:2 AMP, "Beloved, I pray that in every way you may succeed and prosper and *be in good health [physically], just as [I know] your soul prospers [spiritually].*" This God designer life unfolds as you learn to trust and act on God's Word of Life, Jesus. John 1:1-5, "*In the beginning was the Word, and the Word was with God, and the Word was God.* He was with God in the beginning. Through him all things were made; without him nothing was made that has been made. ***In Him was Life***, and that life was the ***Light*** of all humankind. The light shines in the darkness, and the darkness has not overcome it." Verse 14, "The Word became flesh and made his dwelling among us. We have seen his glory, the glory of the one and only Son, who came from the Father, full of grace and truth." Yes, you are born-again and you are in right standing with God; however, ***righteousness is revealed when you believe and become a doer of the Gospel of Jesus Christ.*** Romans 1:16-17 says, "For I am not ashamed of the gospel of Christ, because ***it is the power of God that brings salvation*** to everyone who ***believes***: first to the Jew, then to the Gentile. ***For in the gospel the righteousness of God is revealed***—a righteousness that is by faith from first to last, just as it is written: "The righteous will live by faith." You must lay hold on and possess this peace Jesus died to give you. Keep your mind stayed on Him. He is the Prince of Peace; as Isaiah 26:3 says. "You will keep in perfect peace those whose minds are steadfast because ***they trust in you***." Go ahead, let your expression of joy burst forth because God has already answered your scriptural prayers with a ***yes.*** Your job is to say ***amen!*** "If you remain in me and my words remain in you, ***ask whatever you wish, and it will be done for you***. This is to my Father's glory, that you bear much fruit, ***showing yourselves to be my disciples***. As the Father has loved me, so have I loved you. Now remain in my love. If you keep my commands, you will remain in my love, just as I have kept my Father's commands and remain in his love. *I have told you this so that my joy may be in you and that your joy may be complete.* My command is this: Love each other as I have loved you," John 15:7-12 says.

Your **church court** is there, holding your hand as you work out your salvation. When I reviewed the deeds of the flesh vs the benefits of the life of God's Holy Spirit living in me, I really wanted to **take off** those dirty spiritual clothes of sexual immorality and drunkenness. I wanted to burn them in the fire of the Holy Spirit working in me. I have **put on** my royal outfit, my garments of salvation and my robe of righteousness. As natural clothes cover your body, you should let righteousness, believing the Gospel of Jesus Christ, cover your soul, your thoughts, your will, your words, and your deeds. Get your soul restored by renewing your mind. Die to sins, come alive unto the righteousness of Jesus Christ being revealed in your life; *"by his wounds you have been healed*. For you were like sheep going astray, but *now you have returned to the Shepherd and Overseer of your souls."* (Romans 12:1-3 and 1st Peter 2:24-25.) If you forgot what sin is, take another look at the scriptures defining it. 1st John 5:17, "All wrongdoing is sin, and there is sin that does not lead to death." James 4:17 states, "If anyone, then, knows the good they ought to do and doesn't do it, it is sin for them." Romans 14:23 AMP, "Whatever is not from faith is sin [whatever is done with doubt is sinful]." "Everyone who sins is breaking God's law, for all sin is contrary to the law of God." In James 2:8 we read, "Thou shalt **love thy neighbor as thyself**," this is the "**Royal Law**." "Love does no harm to a neighbor. **Therefore, love is the fulfillment of the law.**" (Romans 13:10) This is how we know who the children of God are and who the children of the devil are: anyone who does not do what is right is not God's child, nor is anyone who does not love their brother and sister. 1st John 3:10 says, "You have to choose to come to the place where you love the Lord your God, first, by obedience to Him. That obedience to Him, in turn will allow you to love your neighbor....as yourself." Matthew 22:36-39 AMP asks, "'Teacher, which is the greatest commandment in the Law?' And Jesus replied to him, "You shall love the Lord your God with all your heart and with all your soul and with all your mind. This is the first and greatest commandment. The second is like it, you shall love your neighbor as yourself.'" You are to unselfishly seek the best or higher good for others. Galatians 5:13-18 says, "...do not use your freedom to indulge the flesh; rather, serve one another humbly in love. **For the entire law is fulfilled in keeping this one command: 'Love your neighbor as yourself.'** If you bite and devour each other, watch out or you will be destroyed by each other. So, I say, walk by the Spirit, and you will not gratify the desires of the flesh. For the flesh desires what is contrary to the Spirit, and the Spirit what is contrary to the flesh. They conflict with each other, so that you are not to do whatever you want. But if the Spirit leads you, (the Word of God in your thoughts, words, and deeds) you are not under the law of sin and death." A law is a system of rules which a particular community recognizes as regulating the actions of its members and which may be enforced by imposing penalties. The law in the Old Testament for God's people was the Ten Commandments. In the New Testament the *"Royal Law"* for God's people is *the law of the "Love of God."* A command is a special specific authoritative order or instruction. We are *commanded* to walk in love. It fulfills all the laws of the Ten Commandments. The *Law of the Spirit of Life in Christ* frees you from the *Law of sin and death* (Romans 8:2). Both are laws. Choose one or the other; they work for everyone the same way all the time. I needed to rid myself of some dirty spiritual clothes if I were to possess my inheritance of salvation in the Kingdom of God. The warnings are noted in Galatians 5:19, "I warn you, as I did before, that those who live like this will not inherit the kingdom of God."

Fornicating with those strong, healthy, sexy men was a no-no. The intoxication had to go, too. I was biblically taught how to manage fornication. I am instructed to get married to a Godly man according to 1st Corinthians 7:9 AMP, "But if they do not have [sufficient] self-control, they should marry; for it is better to marry than to burn with passion." I was biblically taught how to pray and ask God for a Godly husband. The Holy Spirit pointed him out to me in church one Sunday. Alcohol and cigarettes, however, were another story. I did not mind having a cocktail after work and cigarettes usually went along with it. I tried for many years to kick the cigarette habit. The alcohol I never saw as a real problem, other than at times I would get so tipsy I could not drive. I wanted to get rid of both. Someone at my church told me I could get prayed for and the Lord would heal me of both. I asked for prayer, and they bound the alcohol and nicotine spirit, cast it out, and it left me. I have never had another drink or cigarette since, and have no desire for either one. I was healed! Just like that! That really opened my eyes to the power of what the Lord could do in my life. I was glad to get rid of those dirty spiritual clothes. I recently met a girl I ministered to in this area and led to the Lord. She said she was a recovering acholic and had taken classes that would have you to continually call yourself a recovering alcoholic. I said to her, "You are either an alcoholic or not." If I recall correctly, she had not had a drink for many, many, many years. Yet she still called herself a recovering alcoholic. If you are not blue, you just are not blue. If you do not drink alcohol anymore, you are not an alcoholic. You are not still recovering, you are healed. Just because I used to get intoxicated in the past does not make me recovering forever. I am healed! I explained to her that when you get born again, all your sins are washed away, and God does not remember any of them. I told her to start seeing herself the way God sees her, washed clean by the Blood of Jesus. A newborn baby does not have a past. A newly born-again child of God does not have a sin past. The sin nature is gone. You have become a new creation in Christ Jesus. However, if some of those deeds of the flesh, those dirty spiritual clothes, are still trying to hang in the closet of your mind, your job is to change and *put on your royal wardrobe*. 2nd Corinthians 10:5, "Casting down imaginations, and every high thing that exalted itself against the knowledge of God and bringing into captivity every thought to the obedience of Christ." When you change your thinking and clothe your mind with God's righteous thoughts, those dirty spiritual clothes will get washed clean by the Blood of the Lamb and the word of your testimony. "You will be made new in the attitude of your minds as you *put on* the new self, created to be like God in true righteousness and holiness. (Ephesians 4:23-24) Colossians 3:5-10 states, "*Put to death,* (stop it) therefore, whatever belongs to your earthly nature: sexual immorality, impurity, lust, evil desires, and greed, which is idolatry. *Because of these, the wrath of God is coming.* You used to walk in these ways, in the life you once lived. But now you must also rid yourselves of all such things as these: anger, rage, malice, slander, and filthy language from your lips. Do not lie to each other, since you have taken off your old self with its practices and have *put on the new self, which is being renewed in knowledge in the image of its Creator*." (Don't forget you have a spiritual garment called praise.

CHURCH COURT

Praise can release the joy of the Lord and the peace of God into your heart and mind. In Philippians 4:4-7 the Apostle Paul said, "Rejoice in the Lord always. I will say it again: Rejoice! ...be anxious for nothing but by prayer, supplication with thanksgiving let your request be known unto God. And the peace of God, which transcends all understanding, will guard your hearts and your minds in Christ Jesus." I encourage you to put on the garment of praise for the spirit of heaviness. You can praise God in many ways, such as singing psalms and hymns and spiritual songs, making melody in your heart unto the Lord. Don't be afraid to turn up the praise really loud. Read Psalms 149 and 150. This will help you focus and anchor your thinking on the scripture answer to your trivial dispute found on page (2) of your trivial dispute Victory Journal

I would tell my testimony to people who were bound up with addictive spirits and ask them if they wanted to be set free. Some would say yes; some would say no. One person told me they would like to get rid of cigarettes but not alcohol. I think that same person lost the battle with alcohol, and they ended up dying early. Remember, **YOU must put on** your new royal robe of righteousness by believing the truth that is in Jesus. **Put on** your garments of salvation by your faithful obedience to King Jesus, who is the Lord your God. If you do not see any signs of the fruit of the Holy Spirit manifesting in your life, check to see what is in your spiritual wardrobe. What are you meditating on day and night? You will be transformed by changing your thinking. Romans 12:2, "Do not conform to the pattern of this world but be transformed by the renewing of your mind. Then you will be able to test and approve what God's will is—*his good, pleasing, and perfect will.*" Please understand, God is not going to make you do anything. *He said if you love Him, you will obey Him.* Go ahead and apply your three-step trivial dispute resolution salvation plan He has so graciously supplied you with. Psalms 91:14-16 says, "'Because he loves me,' says the Lord, 'I will rescue him; I will protect him, for he acknowledges my name. He will call on me, and I will answer him; I will be with him in trouble, I will deliver him and honor him. *With long life I will satisfy him and show him my salvation.*'" The Spirit of God inside you is a do right spirit, but your old way of thinking and doing things can block your "Royal" view sometimes. Let's repeat God's thoughts about you, which are spelled out in Jeremiah 29:11, "'For I know the plans I have for you,' declares the Lord, '*plans to prosper you* and not to harm you, plans to give you hope and a future.'" In 3rd John 2:1-2, "Dear friend, *I pray that you may enjoy good health and that all may go well with you*, even as your soul is getting along well." You are not alone; you have a helper called the Holy Spirit. Remember, your inheritance in the Kingdom of God is righteousness, peace, and joy, *in the Holy Spirit.* God has given us the sweet Holy Spirit to help us accomplish this beautiful peaceful life He designed for us "But when he, the Spirit of truth comes, he will guide you into all the truth. He will not speak on his own; he will speak only what he hears, and he will tell you what is yet to come. He will glorify me because it is from me that he will receive what he will make known to you. All that belongs to the Father is mine. That is why I said the Spirit will receive from me that he will make known to you." (John 16:13-15) The Holy Spirit will comfort you, counsel you, lead you and guide you into **all the truth**. Always ask the Holy Spirit for help in everything you do. He will help you live right if you let Him lead and guide you. Remember, it is your choice whether you follow the leadership of the Holy Spirit or not. Ephesians 4:30-32 says, "Do not grieve the Holy Spirit of God, with whom you were sealed for the day of redemption. Get rid of all bitterness, rage and anger, brawling, and slander, along with every form of malice. Be kind and compassionate to one another, forgiving each other, just as in Christ God forgave you." James 3:13-16 MSG, "Do you want to be counted wise, to build a reputation for wisdom? Here is what you do: Live well, live wisely, live humbly. ***It is the way you live, not the way you talk, that counts***. Mean-spirited ambition isn't wisdom. Boasting that you are wise isn't wisdom. Twisting the truth to make yourselves sound wise isn't wisdom. It's the furthest thing from wisdom—it is animal cunning, devilish plotting. Whenever you're trying to look better than others or get the better of others, things fall apart and everyone ends up at the others' throats. Real wisdom, God's wisdom, begins with a holy life and is characterized by getting along with others. It is gentle and reasonable, overflowing with mercy and blessings, not hot one day and cold the next, not two-faced. You can develop a healthy, robust community that lives right with God and enjoy its results only if you *do the hard work of getting along with each other, treating each other with dignity and honor.*"

Trust me, it is much easier to follow Jesus! I did not like being sad and unloved. When you think wrong and speak wrong, you end up doing the wrong thing. By your own choice you separate yourself from the Life of God. You deceive yourself into thinking you can make your life right without God. Proverbs 14:12, "There is a way that appears to be right, but in the end, it leads to death." Having a lot of fancy things and big titles do not give you peace, without God. Proverbs10:22 says, "*The blessing of the LORD brings wealth,* without painful toil for it." You must be a doer of His Word to possess your inheritance of salvation, healing in every area of your life. Follow the King's command! It is the law! Genesis 1:26 says God created you in His image and likeness. We follow God's example, therefore, as dearly loved children and walk in the way of love, just as Christ loved us.

Learn what God has to say about your trivial disputes, then make your scriptural prayer request accordingly. Stay focused by thanking and praising God that He heard your prayer and granted it. If you believe that, you will **ACT** accordingly, and your trivial dispute will be resolved. If you are in *church court*, the mediators will give you the correct scriptures to pray and meditate on so you can do them. Loving unlovable people was difficult for me early on. The more I practice walking in the Love of God, the better I am getting at it. If you have not gotten to *church court* yet and you do not know what scriptures to apply to step 1 and Step 2 of the dispute resolution plans, ask God for them. James 1:5-8 tells us, "If any of you lacks wisdom, you should ask God, who gives generously to all without finding fault, and it will be given to you. But when you ask, you must believe and not doubt, because the one who doubts is like a wave of the sea, blown and tossed by the wind. That person should not expect to receive anything from the Lord. Such a person is *double-minded and unstable in all they do.*" God will give you the answer to your trivial dispute. You should write those scriptures out on three-by-five cards and take them with you when you go to resolve your dispute with the person that harmed you. Colossians 3:12-14, "Therefore, as God's chosen people, holy and dearly loved, *clothe yourselves with compassion, kindness, humility, gentleness, and patience. Bear with each other and forgive one another if any of you has a grievance against someone. Forgive as the Lord forgave you*. And over all these virtues put on love, which binds them all together in perfect unity." Ephesians 4:22-24 says, "You were taught, with regard to your former way of life, to put off your old self, which is being corrupted by its deceitful desires; to **be made new in the attitude of your minds; and to put on the new self, created to be like God in true righteousness and holiness**."

Your plan was not working, was it? The Creator of the universe is telling you, He made you and He designed the master salvation plan to save you from sin and death. It is written down in black and white and red. The Holy Bible! Read it! Study it like you did your ABCs and 1-2-3s, then you will be able to do it! In Isaiah 55 and James 1 God says your actions will follow your thoughts. James 3:13-18, "**Who is wise and understanding among you? Let them show it by their good life, by deeds done** in the humility that comes from wisdom. But if you harbor bitter envy and selfish ambition in your hearts, do not boast about it or deny the truth. Such 'wisdom' does not come down from heaven but is earthly, unspiritual, demonic. For where you have envy and selfish ambition, there you find disorder and every evil practice. But the wisdom that comes from heaven is first of all pure, then peace-loving, considerate, submissive, full of mercy and good fruit, impartial and sincere. **Peacemakers who sow in peace reap a harvest of righteousness**." **A long, pleasant life with peaceful paths filled with riches and honor: it is all yours for loving the Lord your God and obeying Him, and loving your neighbor as yourself.**

If you are recently born again or even if you are well

along in your spiritual growth, get busy and resolve your trivial disputes. Go ahead, start with the three steps dispute resolution plan found in Matthew 18:15-17. Do not quit on God, your church, your family, or yourself. God knows how to get things worked out; trust Him by your obedience. Your *church court* will help you. In my prolonged process of trying to resolve my trivial marital dispute, I realized I had no idea what God had to say about Godly marriages. But, when I went to the pastor and found out what the Holy Bible had to say, I was willing to put it into practice. *Church court* is there because **God loves you and He wants you healed.** If you know the right thing to do and you do not do it, well, that is called sin, and the wrath of God comes upon the children of disobedience. According to 1st Thessalonians 5:9-10, your destination in the Kingdom of God is salvation, not wrath. "If we confess our sins, he is faithful and just and will forgive us our sins and purify us from all unrighteousness. (1st John 1:9). "Therefore confess your sins to each other and pray for each other **so that you may be healed**. "The prayer of a righteous person is effective and powerful." (James 5:16) ***Receive your inheritance, your salvation, your healing right now!*** Take step number one; go to the person that offended you with your scriptures and begin the process of resolving your trivial disputes. If they are dead and no longer on the earth; just say, "Lord, I forgive them, I let it go right now. Cleanse me and purify me for your glory. Do not stop until you have **Victory!**

CHAPTER SIX

The Judge's Character, Mediation Process, Renumeration, and the Law

Character and Qualifications

The mediating judges must be able to teach and have Godly character. According to the scripture in Ephesians 4:11-16, *"So Christ himself gave the apostles, the prophets, the evangelists, the pastors and teachers, to equip his people for works of service*, so that the body of Christ may be built up until we all reach unity in the faith and in the knowledge of the Son of God and become mature, attaining to the whole measure of the fullness of Christ. Then we will no longer be infants, tossed back and forth by the waves, and blown here and there by every wind of teaching and by the cunning and craftiness of people in their deceitful scheming. Instead, speaking the truth in love, we will grow to become in every respect the mature body of him who is the head, that is, Christ. From him the whole body, joined and held together by every supporting ligament, grows, and builds itself up in love, as each part does its work." 1st Timothy 3:1-7 says, "Here is a trustworthy saying: Whoever aspires to be an overseer desires a noble task. Now the overseer is to be above reproach, faithful to his wife, temperate, self-controlled, respectable, hospitable, *able to teach,* not given to drunkenness, not violent but gentle, not quarrelsome, not a lover of money. He must manage his own family well and see that his children obey him, and he must do so in a manner worthy of full respect. (*If anyone does not know how to manage his own family, how can he take care of God's church?*) He must not be a recent convert, or he may become conceited and fall under the same judgment as the devil. He must also have a good reputation with outsiders, so that he will not fall into disgrace and into the devil's trap."

This looks like a fulltime job for the appointed officials that are to serve as judges for God's people. We also see that this was not just a suggestion, but a command from God. This is not a one-man job and is not a position for deacons, as there is no requirement for the deacons to be able to teach, only to assist the overseeing elders, the five-fold ministry. It is also not a job for a new believer. We see in 1st Corinthians 6:1-10 that these judges should be wise enough in the Holy Scriptures to be able to judge trivial disputes among God's people. Their wisdom is based on their knowledge and experience in the Word of God. ***Not only preaching and teaching needs to be done, but there is also the job of rebuking, correcting, and training in righteousness involved*** according to 2nd Timothy 3:16. God Himself placed these five-fold preaching and teaching gifts in **His Church** for a specific reason: to train God's people up to maturity in the faith and the agape love. It is necessary to preach and tell God's people what God said about living right. However, to teach them how to do it is a training process. Living a life free from repetitive sinning is available to everyone who believes and enters the Kingdom of God by the spiritual new birth. Once you are born again, the royal training for reigning as King's Kids has begun. No doubt, along the way you will run into more than one trivial dispute with your brothers and sisters in the Lord. Faith worketh by love. No love in action, no faith working which no doubt is hindering your maturity. However, that is no reason to abort your training nor turn back to the ways of the world. ***Understand the value of solving your trivial disputes so you can enjoy your good life in Christ here in the now and eternity with Him forever.*** Teaching involves explaining and showing you how to do it, and training will give you an opportunity to practice doing the right thing. James 3:18 AMP, "And the seed whose fruit is righteousness (spiritual maturity) is sown in peace by those who make peace [by actively encouraging goodwill between individuals]." Practice! Practice! Practice! The more you practice settling your trivial disputes quickly, the easier it becomes. No need to let it go on for years and years like I did. Mark 4:24 tells us the measure you hear, study, and practice God's Word is the measure of righteous return you will get. Maturity comes from exercising your faith and walking in love. 1st Timoty 4:8 AMP, "For physical training is of some value, but godliness (spiritual training) is of value in everything *and* in every way since it holds promise for the present life and for the life to come." (Hebrews 5:12-14 EXB) says, "By now you should be teachers, but you need someone to teach you again the first lessons [elementary truths; basic principles] of God's message [revelation; oracles]. You still need the teaching that is like milk. You are not ready for solid food. Anyone who lives on milk is still a baby and knows nothing about [or is unskilled/inexperienced with] right teaching [or the message about righteousness]. *But solid food is for those who are grown up [mature]. They are mature enough [... who through practice/exercise have trained their faculties/ senses] to know the difference between good and evil."* "Go out and train everyone you meet, far and near, in this way of life, marking them by baptism in the threefold name: Father, Son, and Holy Spirit. Then **instruct them in the practice** of all I have commanded you. I will be with you as you do this, day after day after day, right up to the end of the age." (Matthew 28:18-20) *Church court* would be a full-time job for more than one person. It is for those who not only can preach (tell you) but also teach (show you how to do it) and who are wise enough in the scriptures to be able to patiently "correct (those who err in doctrine or behavior), warn [(those who sin], exhort and encourage [those who are growing toward spiritual maturity], with inexhaustible patience and [faithful] teaching."

Sometimes Christians turn back to the world's secular ways and abort their walk with the Lord because of offence or disappointments. A brother or sister in the Lord has harmed them in some way and they do not know how to get that trivial dispute resolved. Sometimes even if you go to the person who offended you and you scripturally and peacefully point out the wrong they have done to you, they will not admit it nor humble themselves to forgive or repent. If you are not skilled in repentance and forgiveness, you may live with that bitterness in your heart for years. You may assume all Christians are that way. This anger, agitation, annoyance, and disappointment at the Christian offender can really be a hinderance to your love walk, if you let it. You may feel cheated, abused, and rejected. That is the way I felt when the Lord told me to go love my husband the way He loved me. I felt cheated. I argued with the Lord in my prayer closet and said, "No, Lord, You do not understand. It is not me; it is him who is in the wrong." Here I was trying to do the right thing, and in my opinion my husband was the one that was out of line. Then the Lord corrects me and tells me to get up and go love him the way "He" loves me. Walking in the Agape love of God does not mean you are condoning the person's ugly, sinful behavior, nor does it mean you should stay in abusive relationships. We see instructions in the God kind of love in Romans 12:9-21, "Love must be sincere. Hate what is evil; cling to what is good. *Be devoted to one another in love. Honor one another above yourselves*. Never be lacking in zeal, but keep your spiritual fervor, serving the Lord. Be joyful in hope, patient in affliction, faithful in prayer. Share with the Lord's people who are in need. Practice hospitality. Bless those who persecute you; bless and do not curse. Rejoice with those who rejoice; mourn with those who mourn. Live in harmony with one another. Do not be proud but be willing to associate with people of low position. Do not be conceited. *Do not repay anyone evil for evil. Be careful to do what is right in the eyes of everyone. If it is possible, as far as it depends on you, live at peace with everyone. Do not take revenge, my dear friends, but leave room for God's wrath, for it is written: 'It is mine to avenge; I will repay,' says the Lord.* On the contrary: 'If your enemy is hungry, feed him; if he is thirsty, give him something to drink. In doing this, you will heap burning coals on his head.' **Do not be overcome by evil but overcome evil with good."** This is where your humble submission in obedience to King Jesus, God's Word of life and love, can heal you and your trivial dispute. Otherwise, the anger and disappointment in an unforgiving, un-repentant heart could cause sickness and disease in you, thereby stunting your spiritual growth and possibly causing an early death. 1st Corinthians 11: 30 tells us, **"Some are weak, some are sick and some die early because they don't decern the body of Christ and examine themselves** in times of communion." If you are spiritually weak, start exercising your faith and love walk. What you do to your brothers and sisters in the Lord, you are doing to Christ Jesus. The Church is the Bride of Christ, His body, and you cannot separate the two. The head belongs to the body and the body to the head. You mess with the Church, God's people, you are messing with Christ.

Not too long ago, my husband and I were driving down the highway and we had a super big, heated blow out over a ridiculously small matter. He wanted to know which way he should turn at the upcoming traffic light, a right or a left. I said go left, he said no, he thought he should go right. I said, "No, honey, go left" ....and on and on we went until we were screaming at each other at the top of our lungs. The atmosphere was filled with strife. Well, he listened to me, and it was the wrong turn. "You're crazy," he said. "I told you I was right." Oh! I abruptly came to my spiritual senses and told my husband, "I am sorry, I was wrong and please forgive me for screaming and getting into strife." Then I told him he also needed to repent and say he was sorry for screaming at me and calling me crazy. I said, "I rebuke you in Jesus' Name. How dare you call me crazy? I have the mind of Christ and the Holy Spirit is active and alive in me; I am one with the Lord. There is nothing crazy about either one of them, so you cannot call me that. I admit I made a mistake, and I said I am sorry. Now it is your turn to say you are sorry." He was really heated and revved up for some odd reason, and he refused to forgive me, and he refused to repent (change his thought, words, and deeds to what is right). Ephesians 4:29-32 MSG says, "**Watch the way you talk. Let nothing foul or dirty come out of your mouth.** Say only what helps, each word a gift. Do not grieve God. Do not break his heart. His Holy Spirit, moving and breathing in you, is the most intimate part of your life, making you fit for himself. Do not take such a gift for granted. Make a clean break with all cutting, backbiting, profane talk. Be gentle with one another, sensitive. **Forgive one another as quickly** and thoroughly as God in Christ forgave you." I said to my husband, "According to the Bible (Mark 11:25) you must forgive me, or God will not forgive you. You should also repent and only call me what God calls me."1st Peter 3:7 says, "Husbands, in the same way be considerate as you live with your wives and treat them with respect as the weaker partner and as heirs with you of the gracious gift of life, so that nothing will hinder your prayers. Wash her with the water of the Word." He refused both! "Well, I said, I just won't stay around anyone who is going to call me ugly names." "Good, then leave, when are you leaving?" he said. "I get the house," he said. The conversation was getting very ugly and harsh in the car, so I turned the Christian radio station on to try to clear the air. When things calmed down a little, I said again, "You should repent for calling me bad names and you need to forgive me for my ugly behavior." Then I said to him, "I am trying to practice the three-step dispute resolution plan with you. If you are not going to cooperate and forgive and repent, I will have to get me two or three Christian witnesses and my Scriptures and come back and try again to resolve this with you." He was still extremely hot under the collar for some reason. He said, "I don't care how many witnesses you get; you won't find me." I said, "Well, when I do find you, we will have to go to our church court to resolve it."

"You don't have a *church court*," he said, "and you cannot make me go to *church court*. I will just move on to another church and no one will ever know we had a trivial dispute." Finally, after what seemed like an extraordinarily long lull of silence, he came to his spiritual senses and said he was sorry for calling me bad names and getting into strife, and he forgave me for my ruckus. We finally kissed and made up.

That all happened in the space of approximately one-half hour. What really surprised me was, in such a brief period of time, how angry and out of the agape love walk we had gotten. In his conversation he had gone off with the house to somewhere that I would not be able to find him. In the same conversation I was left holding the bag to try to find him and take him to *church court* and retrieve the house. I thought about that blow up long afterward. It is amazing how trivial things can blow up way out of proportion and grow into grandiose things, separating families and relationships. I said, "Lord... what about that? Those Christian people who are too proud to humble themselves and who do not want to forgive and repent? Those Christians who just walk off and leave the whole trivial dispute unresolved and move on to another church or no church?" The scripture that came to my mind in 2nd Timothy 3:1-5 says, "But mark this: There will be terrible times in the last days. People will be lovers of themselves, lovers of money, boastful, proud, abusive, disobedient to their parents, ungrateful, unholy, **without love, unforgiving, slanderous, without self-control**, brutal, not lovers of the good, treacherous, rash, conceited, lovers of pleasure rather than lovers of God— having a form of godliness but denying its power. Have nothing to do with such people." And then in 2nd Timothy 4:3-4 AMP, "For the time will come when people will not tolerate sound doctrine and accurate instruction [that challenges them with God's truth]; but wanting to have their ears tickled [with something pleasing], they will accumulate for themselves [many] teachers [one after another, chosen] to satisfy their own desires and to support the errors they hold, and *will turn their ears away from the truth and will wander off into myths and man-made fictions* [and will accept the unacceptable]." According to this scripture, some Christians may be too proud to walk in love and practice forgiveness and repentance. Their pride would stop them from possessing their inheritance of salvation, the healing that is needed in that area of their life. They will be in the Kingdom of God but not possess the peace and joy and things made right. In order for the teaching on *church courts* to be effective, this point must be expressed clearly. Pride can stop you from working out your plan of salvation. We must learn to be quick to submit to the Word of God, in Matthew 18:15-17 and resolve your trivial dispute. Jesus said in Luke 6:46 AMP, "Why do you call Me, 'Lord, Lord,' and do not practice what I tell you?"

It does not matter where you run to, your unforgiven and unrepentant heart will still be there when you get there. It is like you are carrying around a vial of poison everywhere you go, and it is slowly leaking and killing you from the inside out. It is robbing you of your joy and peace.

Your official overseers, leaders, elders, those who are wise enough in the five-fold ministry with the gift of speaking, *the capable leaders in your church court are there to help you*. If you cannot get the trivial dispute resolved on your own in step one and two, do not hesitate; go straight to step three, your *church court*. They are not there to condemn you but to build you up and encourage you as you grow up spiritually. They are there to assist you in getting those trivial disputes peacefully resolved so that you can move on to spiritual maturity. Then the Beautiful Bride of Christ, the City on the Hill, shining brightly in the darkest of nights, we, God's people, can all go to our homes satisfied, possessing our inheritance, salvation, walking in perfect health and wealth in the Kingdom of God experiencing righteousness, peace and joy in the Holy Spirit, thy Kingdom come, thy will be done *on earth as it is in heaven.*

The Mediation Process

Step One - Preparation
After the disputing parties have gone online to **churchcourt.org** and filled in the proper forms (the summons and complaint and the answer and all

CHURCH COURT

discoveries), they should submit them electronically to their church court clerk. The court clerk should open an electronic file on each case that comes in for review. Once the church court clerk has collected all the supporting and necessary forms and made sure they were properly filled out with the correct supporting scriptures, the file should be submitted to the mediating judges (minimum three) for review and a scriptural resolution plan of action should be decided on to resolve the trivial dispute. Once the case is ready to be heard, the court clerk who keeps the hearing calendar should schedule a hearing date and notify all parties by certified mail when to appear in their church court.

Step Two – The Hearing

Once the case is heard, the mediating judges should supply the appropriate scriptural plan of action for each trivial dispute. The court orders should be given to the disputing parties, explained both verbally and in writing. Be sure both parties sign off that they have received the instructions and understand what they are to do. If possible, there should be verbal confession of forgiveness and repentance recorded at the hearing. A healing probationary period should be given for deeds of repentance and forgiveness to take place. The court should request quarterly progress reports and review them with accountability comments returned to the parties of the case. The sheep should know that the shepherds care about their spiritual health.

Step Three -Restoration

Once the parties of the lawsuit have corrected their behavior and the trivial dispute has been resolved, the case should be closed. If for any reason the parties had to stop serving the congregation with their ministerial gifts, they should now be restored. God does not remember their sins, and neither should anyone else. It is particularly important that there have been clear deeds of repentance and forgiveness, and the fruit thereof should show up in a changed, restored person's thoughts, words, and deeds. Do not hesitate to extend the healing probation time if needed. This probation is meant to be a method used to deal with offenders by allowing them to remain in the fellowship if the *church court* conditions are followed.

Step Four – Expel

If there has been no compliance in the probationary time allotted by the *church court*, the next step would be to expel them from the sheepfold. They will be treated like a tax collector or a pagan, since there is no submission to the Word of God and the instructions of the mediating elders in the *church court*. All cases should be treated with the same respect to prevent unfair practices and favoritism. Send a certified letter stating the reason for the expulsion. They are free then to revert to 1st Corinthians 6:4, "Therefore, if you have disputes about such matters, do you **ask for a ruling from those whose way of life is scorned in the church?"**

Renumeration

"The elders, (or the five-fold ministers), who are directing the affairs of the church well, **are worthy of double honor, especially those whose work is preaching and teachin**g. For Scripture says, 'Do not muzzle an ox while it is treading out the grain,' and 'The worker deserves his wage.'" Pay the mediating judges well. (1st Timothy 5:17-18)

The people of the church must be taught to give their tithes and offerings. Malachi 3:8-12 points out they cannot be God-robbers and be blessed. "Will a mere mortal rob God? Yet you rob me. But you ask, 'How are we robbing you?' In tithes and offerings. You are under a curse—your whole nation—because you are robbing me. Bring the whole tithe into the storehouse, so that there may be food in my house. **Test Me in this**, says the Lord Almighty, and see if I will not throw open the flood gates of heaven and pour out so much blessing that there will not be room enough to store it. I will prevent pests from devouring your crops, and the vines in your fields will not drop their fruit before it is ripe, says the Lord Almighty. Then all the nations will call you blessed, for yours will be a delightful land." Notice the instruction. is to **bring the tithe,** not send it. If you bring it, you will more than likely sit and listen to the Word of God and get blessed. You will get a good spoken Word at the exact time that you need it. Abraham, our father of faith, gave a tithe (one tenth) to Melchizedek, the Hight Priest of the Most High God. Melchizedek, the greater blessed the lesser. We see Jesus as our High Priest in the order of Melchizedek in Hebrews 7:17, "For it is attested [by God] of Him, you are a priest forever in the order of Melchizedek." Then in Galatians 3:7-9 & 29 we are to "Understand, then, that those who have faith are children of Abraham." Scripture foresaw that God would justify the Gentiles by faith, and announced the gospel in advance to Abraham: "All nations will be blessed through you." So those who rely on faith are blessed along with Abraham, the man of faith. "If you belong to Christ, then you are Abraham's seed, and heirs according to the promise." Jesus, He is the greater who blesses us today, the Seed of Abraham. Even to this day, the one who gets blessed pays tithes to the one who is blessing you. Jesus blesses us through those who are gifted to peach and teach the gospel. The tithe (10% of your income) is holy and belongs to our great High Priest, Jesus Christ. It belongs to those who are preaching and teaching the Gospel, the overseeing elders of your church. We are instructed in Galatians 6:6, "the one who is taught the word [of God] is to share all good things with his teacher [contributing to his spiritual and material support]."

Offerings are for the needs of the saints. Ephesians 4:28 puts it like this, "Anyone who has been stealing must steal no longer, but must work, doing something useful with their own hands, that they may have something to share with those in need." The needs of the saints are described in Matthew 25:37-40, "Then the righteous will answer him, 'Lord, when did we see you hungry and feed you, or thirsty and give you something to drink? When did we see you a stranger and invite you in, or needing clothes and clothe you? When did we see you sick or in prison and go to visit you?' The King will reply, '**Truly I tell you, whatever you did for one of the least of these brothers and sisters of mine, you did for me.**'" The tithe is set at 10% by God, but the offerings are set by you, any amount over and above the tithe. 2nd Corinthians 9:6-end says, "Remember this: Whoever sows sparingly will also reap sparingly, and whoever sows generously will also reap generously. Each of you should give what you have decided in your heart to give, not reluctantly or under compulsion, for God loves a cheerful giver. And God is able to bless you abundantly, so that in all things at all times, having all that you need, you will abound in every good work. As it is written: 'They have freely scattered their gifts to the poor; their righteousness endures forever.' Now he who supplies seed to the Sower and bread for food will also supply and increase your store of seed and will enlarge the harvest of your righteousness. You will be enriched in every way so that you can be generous on every occasion, and through us your generosity will result in thanksgiving to God. *This service that you perform is not only supplying the needs of the Lord's people but is also overflowing in many expressions of thanks to God*. Because of the service by which you have proved yourselves, others will praise God for the obedience that accompanies your confession of the gospel of Christ, and for your generosity in sharing with them and with everyone else. And in their prayers for you their hearts will go out to you, because of the surpassing grace God has given you. Thanks be to God for his indescribable gift!" It is explained to us in 1st Corinthians 9:7-11, "Don't you know that those who serve in the temple get their food from the temple, and *that those who serve at the altar share in what is offered on the altar*? In the same way, *the Lord has commanded that those who preach the gospel should receive their living from the gospel*. "Who serves as a soldier at his own expense? Who plants a vineyard (apostles and evangelists usually plant churches) and does not eat its grapes? Who tends to the flock (the teaching and preaching overseeing elders of your church the pastors are to watch over their flock and train them up to do the work of the ministry) and does not drink milk? Do I say this merely on human authority? Doesn't the Law say the same thing? For it is written in the Law of Moses: 'Do not muzzle an ox while it is treading out the grain.' Is it about oxen that God is concerned? Surely, *he says this for us, doesn't he? Yes, this was written for us, because whoever plows and threshes should be able to do so in the hope of sharing in the harvest. If we have sown spiritual seed among you, is it too much if we reap a material harvest from you."*

Check the giving records. Make sure the disputing parties understand the reasons for tithes and offerings and especially so if the trivial disputes are over money. If there has been no giving money seed to the needs of the saints, there obviously is nothing for God to multiply. 2nd Corinthians 8:7-9 says, "But since you excel in everything—in faith, in speech, in knowledge, in complete earnestness and in the love we have kindled in you—*see that you also excel in this grace of giving*. I am not commanding you, but I want to *test the sincerity of your love* by comparing it with the earnestness of others." When I worked in the real estate salesroom, my paycheck would reflect my skills. So goes ministry. Preach, teach, cast out devils, heal the sick, rebuke, correct and train up the children of God in righteousness, to spiritual maturity, with long suffering and patience. Your paycheck should reflect your ministry skills, single honors or double honors.

The Law of God

The Holy Bible is the Law Book. The mediating judges in your *church court* will be skilled in rightly dividing the Word of Truth. The "Royal Law" found in James 2:8 puts all decisions in a nutshell by saying "Love your neighbor as yourself, you are doing right." Romans 13:8-10 says, "Let no debt remain outstanding, except the continuing debt to love one another, for whoever loves others has fulfilled the law. The commandments, 'You shall not commit adultery,' 'You shall not murder,' 'You shall not steal,' 'You shall not covet,' and whatever other command there may be, are summed up in this one command: 'Love your neighbor as yourself.' Love does no harm to a neighbor. Therefore, love is the fulfillment of the law." In Galatians 5:14-15 we read, "For the entire law is fulfilled in keeping this one command: 'Love your neighbor as yourself. If you bite and devour each other, watch out or you will be destroyed by each other." Hebrews 10:26-27) AMP says, "For if we go on willfully and deliberately sinning after receiving the knowledge of the truth, there no longer remains a sacrifice [to atone] for our sins [that is, no further offering to anticipate], but a kind of awful and terrifying expectation of [divine] judgment and the fury of a fire and burning wrath which will consume the adversaries, [those who put themselves

CHURCH COURT

in opposition to God]." With the help of the Holy Spirit, you can say No to all ungodliness.

1st John 3:4-10 reads, "Everyone who sins breaks the law; in fact, sin is lawlessness. *But you know that he appeared so that he might take away our sins. And in him is no sin. No one who lives in him keeps on sinning. No one who continues to sin has either seen him or known him.* Dear children, do not let anyone lead you astray. The one who does what is right is righteous, just as he is righteous. The one who does what is sinful is of the devil, because the devil has been sinning from the beginning. The reason the Son of God appeared was to destroy the devil's work. No one who is born of God will continue to sin, because God's seed remains in them; they cannot go on sinning, because they have been born of God. This is how we know who the children of God are and who the children of the devil are: Anyone who does not do what is right is not God's child, nor is anyone who does not love their brother and sister." Ouch!

CHAPTER SEVEN

Judging the World and Angels

Now, because the **church courts** have done such an excellent job settling the trivial disputes of God's Children, they should be ready and fit for judging the world and angels in the thousand-year millennial reign. 1st Corinthians 6:2-3 AMP, "***Do you not know that the saints (God's people) will [one day] judge the world?*** If the world is to be judged by you, are you not competent to try trivial (insignificant, petty) cases? ***Do you not know that we [believers] will judge angels***? How much more then [as to] matters of this life." Revelations 20:4-6 AMP says, "And ***then I saw thrones, and sitting on them were those to whom judgment [that is, the authority to act as judges] was given.*** And I saw the souls of those who had been beheaded because of their testimony of Jesus and because of the word of God, and those who had refused to worship the beast or his image and had not accepted his mark on their forehead and on their hand; ***and they came to life***

and reigned with Christ for a thousand years. The rest of the dead [the non-believers] did not come to life again until the thousand years were completed. This is the first resurrection. Blessed (happy, prosperous, to be admired) and holy is the person who takes part in the first resurrection. Over these the second death [which is eternal separation from God, the lake of fire] has no power or authority, **but they will be priests of God and of Christ and they will reign with Him a thousand years**." We read in Revelations 5:1, 5-10, "I saw in the right hand of Him who was seated on the throne a scroll written on the inside and on the back, closed and sealed with seven seals... Then one of the [twenty-four] elders said to me, 'Stop weeping! Look closely, the Lion of the tribe of Judah, the Root of David, has overcome and conquered! He can open the scroll and [break] its seven seals.' And there between the throne (with the four living creatures) and among the elders I saw a Lamb (Christ) standing, [bearing scars and wounds] as though it had been slain, with seven horns (complete power) and with seven eyes (complete knowledge), which are the seven Spirits of God who have been sent [on duty] into all the earth. And He came and took the scroll from the right hand of Him who sat on the throne. And when He had taken the scroll, the four living creatures and the twenty-four elders fell down before the Lamb (Christ), each one holding a harp and golden bowls full of fragrant incense,

CHURCH COURT

which are the prayers of the saints (God's people). And they sang a new song [of glorious redemption], saying, Worthy and deserving are You to take the scroll and to break its seals; for You were slain (sacrificed), and with Your blood You purchased people for God from every tribe and language and people and nation. *You have made them to be a kingdom [of royal subjects] and priests to our God; and they will reign on the earth."* Revelation 3:21 AMP, "He who overcomes [the world through believing that Jesus is the Son of God], *I will grant to him [the privilege] to sit beside Me on My throne, as I also overcame and sat down beside My Father on His throne*." Again, in Mathew 19:27-29 AMP, "Then Peter answered Him, saying, 'Look, we have given up everything and followed You [becoming Your disciples and accepting You as Teacher and Lord]; what then will there be for us?' Jesus said to them, 'I assure you and most solemnly say to you, *in the renewal [that is, the Messianic restoration and regeneration of all things] when the Son of Man sits on His glorious throne, you [who have followed Me, becoming My disciples] will also sit on twelve thrones*, judging the twelve tribes of Israel. And everyone who has left houses or brothers or sisters or father or mother or children or farms for My name's sake will receive many times as much and will inherit eternal life.'" This is the Great Reversal: many of the first ending up last, and the last first. Throughout the book of Revelation, we see those who will be judging the world and the angels who were locked up in darkness for the day of judgement. Revelation 5:26 says, "**To the one who is victorious and does my will to the end, I will give authority over the nations—that one 'will rule them with an iron scepter and will dash them to pieces like pottery'—just as I have received authority from my Father.**" Revelations 5:11 tells us, "Whoever has ears, let them hear what the Spirit says to the churches. The one who is victorious will not be hurt at all by the second death." (Remember in Revelation 20 those who made the rapture of the church, or the first resurrection, will not be hurt by the second death, and they will be given thrones and reign with Christ 1000 years.) Revelation 19:5-22 says, "Then a voice came from the throne, saying: 'Praise our God, all you his servants, you who fear him, both great and small! Then I heard what sounded like a great multitude, like the roar of rushing waters and like loud peals of thunder, shouting: 'Hallelujah! For our Lord God Almighty reigns. Let us rejoice and be glad and give him glory!' For the wedding of the Lamb has come, and his bride has made herself ready. Fine linen, bright and clean, was given her to wear. [Fine linen stands for the righteous acts of God's holy people.] Then the angel said to me, 'Write this: Blessed are those who are invited to the wedding supper of the Lamb!' I saw heaven standing open and there before me was a white horse, whose rider is called Faithful and True. With justice he judges and wages war. His eyes are like blazing fire, and on his head are many crowns. He has a name written on him that no one knows but he himself. He is dressed in a robe dipped in blood, and his name is the Word of God. **The armies of heaven were following him, riding on white horses and dressed in fine linen, white and clean.** Coming out of his mouth is a sharp sword with which to strike down the nations. He will rule them with an iron scepter. He treads the winepress of the fury of the wrath of God Almighty. On his robe and on his thigh, he has this name written: KING OF KINGS AND LORD OF LORDS." In Revelation 3:19-22 we see those who will be given the right to sit with the Lord Jesus on His throne. "Those whom I love I rebuke and discipline. So be earnest and repent. Here I am! I stand at the door and knock. If anyone hears my voice and opens the door, I will come in and eat with that person, and they with me. *To the one who is victorious, I will give the right to sit with me on my throne, just as I was victorious and sat down with my Father on His throne. Whoever has ears, let them hear what the Spirit says to the churches.*"

Let us turn up the light in our lamps and let the city on the hill shine brightly in this end time darkness. Matthew 5:13-16, "You are the salt of the earth. But if the salt loses its saltiness, how can it be made salty again? It is no longer good for anything, except to be thrown out and trampled underfoot. You are the light of the world. A town built on a hill cannot be hidden. Neither do people light a lamp and put it under a bowl. Instead, they put it on its stand, and it gives light to everyone in the house. In the same way, let your light shine before others, that they may see your good deeds and glorify your Father in heaven." Let us practice getting our trivial disputes settled quickly, thus allowing our peaceful, joyful, righteous lives to reflect the goodness of God to the dark world. They will be thirsty for what you have, and we will increase the harvest of souls, reconciling the world to God. Get your *church courts* set up. Mediators, be instrumental with a faith-based plan of action to help God's people resolve their trivial disputes quickly and efficiently according to the Royal law of love. It is a gift from God Almighty to be able to go to your home in peace. It is your right, your inheritance, your salvation; the peace of God through Jesus Christ belongs to God's people. Let us be ready to make the first resurrection, wearing white linen, our wedding gowns, thus escaping the second death, the lake of fire. After the wedding supper, let us be ready to come back with Jesus clothed in white linen, to judge the world and the angels that were locked up until the day of judgement, according to 2 Peter 2:4-10. " ***For if God did not spare angels when they sinned, but sent them to hell, putting them in chains of darkness to be held for judgment;*** if he did not spare the ancient world when he brought the flood on its ungodly people, but protected Noah, a preacher of righteousness, and seven others; if he condemned the cities of Sodom and Gomorrah by burning them to ashes, and made them an example of what is going to happen to the ungodly; and if he rescued Lot, a righteous man, who was distressed by the depraved conduct of the lawless (for that righteous man, living among them day after day, was tormented in his righteous soul by the lawless deeds he saw and heard)— if this is so, then the Lord knows how to rescue the godly from trials and to hold the unrighteous for punishment on the day of judgment. This is especially true of those who follow the corrupt desire of the flesh and despise authority."

The beautiful, victorious bride of Christ we are, dressed in our white linen wedding gown, earning the right to sit with King Jesus on His throne when He returns to earth with His army of saints. Because our *church courts* have done such an excellent job of helping God's people settle their trivial disputes, we are honored to be given the authority to rule the nations, reigning with Christ 1000 years. The second death, the lake of fire, was not meant for God's people, the righteous sheep who follow the voice of the Good Shepherd. Your name is not blotted out of the Book of Life, is it? Remember, you can enter the Kingdom of God, and even see all that belongs to you as a child of God, but we shall also possess our life made right, our peace and joy in the Holy Ghost as we diligently work out our salvation by exercising our faith, hope, and love. When you run into a trivial dispute with your brothers and sisters in the Lord, do not turn back to the ways of the world. Learn to use your three-step trivial dispute resolution plan of forgiveness and repentance. Do not allow the devil to steal your inheritance. Settle your trivial disputes quickly. If you do not have a home church with a ***church court***, find one immediately. We all need help growing up spiritually. Ask God where your pastor is, and He will show you. If you already have one, get committed and rooted and serve the Lord with gladness with the gift He gave you to minister to your fellow brothers and sisters. 1st Peter 4:7-11 says, "The end of all things is near. Therefore, be alert and of sober mind so that you may pray. ***Above all, love each other deeply, because love covers over a multitude of sins.*** Offer hospitality to one another without grumbling. ***Each of you should use whatever gift you have received to serve others, as faithful stewards of God's grace in its various forms. If anyone SPEAKS, they should do so as one who speaks the very words of God. If anyone SERVES, they should do so with the strength God provides, so that in all things God may be praised through Jesus Christ.*** To him be the glory and the power for ever and ever. Amen."

Do not give up on God, do not give up on yourself, and do not give up on your natural or spiritual family. Proverbs 3:5-18 reads, "Trust in the Lord with all your heart and lean not on your own understanding; in all your ways submit to him, and he will make your paths straight. Do not be wise in your own eyes; fear the LORD and shun evil. This will bring health to your body and nourishment to your bones. Honor the LORD with your wealth, with the first fruits of all your crops; then your barns will be filled to overflowing, and your vats will brim over with new wine. My son, ***do not despise the Lord's discipline, and do not resent his rebuke, because the Lord disciplines those he loves, as a father the son he delights in.*** Blessed are those who find wisdom, those who gain understanding, for she is more profitable than silver and yields better returns than gold. ***She is more precious than rubies; nothing you desire can compare with her. Long life is in her right hand; in her left hand are riches and honor. Her ways are pleasant ways, and ALL her paths are peace.*** She is a tree of life to those who take hold of her; those who hold her fast will be blessed."

Judgement time reveals all. Hebrews 9:27 states, "As it appointed unto men once to die, but after this the judgement." 2nd Corinthians 5:10, "For ***we (all believers in Christ) must all appear before the judgment seat of Christ, so that each of us may receive what is due us for the things*** done while in the body, whether good or bad." John 5:28-29 says, "Do not be amazed at this, for a time is coming when all who are in their graves will hear his voice and come out—those who have done what is good will rise to live, and those who have done what is evil will rise to be condemned." The unbelievers will have to rise and give an account of their deeds to God after the 1000-year millennial reign of Christ and His Bride. They will go before the Great White Throne of Judgement (Revelation 20). All whose names are not found in the Book of Life will be thrown into the lake of fire with the devil and his angels, the beast, and false prophets.

In Matthew 25:31-34, we see Jesus sitting on His throne rewarding the sheep who followed His voice. He tells them to take their inheritance, the Kingdom prepared for them from the foundation of the world. "My sheep hear my voice, and I know them, and they follow me: And I give unto them eternal life; and they shall never perish, neither shall any man pluck them out of my hand." (See also John 10:27) 1st Thessalonians 4:5 tells us the Church will rise at the trumpet call and meet Jesus in the sky, then according to Matthew 25 there will be a separation of sheep and goats at the judgement seat of Christ. ***After the wedding feast, the Church comes back with Jesus and touches down on the Mount of Olives to judge the nations*** (Jude 1:14). Looks like there was a wedding feast in Matthew 22:11-14, "But when the king came in to see the guests, he noticed a man there who was not wearing wedding clothes. He asked, 'How did you get in here without wedding clothes, friend?' The

CHURCH COURT

man was speechless. Then the king told the attendants, 'Tie him hand and foot, and throw him outside, into the darkness, where there will be weeping and gnashing of teeth.' For many are invited, but few are chosen." (Fine linen stands for the righteous acts of God's holy people, Revelation 19:8). In Zechariah 14:4-5, we see Jesus coming back after the rapture with His Bride. "On that day, his feet will stand on the Mount of Olives, east of Jerusalem, and the Mount of Olives will be split in two from east to west, forming a great valley, with half of the mountain moving north and half moving south. You will flee by my mountain valley, for it will extend to Azel. You will flee as you fled from the earthquake in the days of Uzziah king of Judah. Then the Lord my God will come, and all the Holy Ones with Him." In 2nd Peter 2:8-10, he speaks of Lot who was living in Sodom in Gomorrah, ("For that righteous man, living among them day after day, was tormented in his righteous soul by the lawless deeds he saw and heard)— if this is so, *then the Lord knows how to rescue the godly from trials and to hold the unrighteous for punishment on the day of judgment*. This is especially true of those who follow the corrupt desire of the flesh and despise authority." Then again in Jude 1:14-19 we see Jesus and His Bride, God's people, coming to judge the world, *"and Enoch, the seventh from Adam, prophesied about them: 'See, the Lord is coming with thousands upon thousands of his holy ones to judge everyone, and to convict all of them of all the ungodly acts they have committed in their ungodliness, and of all the defiant words ungodly sinners have spoken against him.*'" These people are grumblers and faultfinders; they follow their own evil desires; they boast about themselves and flatter others for their own advantage. But, dear friends, remember what the apostles of our Lord Jesus Christ foretold. They said to you, "In the last times there will be scoffers who will follow their own ungodly desires." These are the people who divide you, who follow mere natural instincts and do not have the Spirit." In the book of Jude verses 3-7, "Dear friends, although I was very eager to write to you about the salvation we share, I felt compelled to write and urge you to contend for the faith that was once for all entrusted to God's holy people. For certain individuals, whose condemnation was written about long ago have secretly slipped in among you. They are ungodly people, who pervert the grace of our God into a license for immorality and deny Jesus Christ our only Sovereign and Lord. Though you already know all this, I want to remind you that the Lord at one time delivered his people out of Egypt, but later destroyed those who did not believe. *And the angels who did not keep their positions of authority but abandoned their proper dwelling—these he has kept in darkness, bound with everlasting chains for judgment on the great Day.* In a similar way, Sodom and Gomorrah and the surrounding towns gave themselves up to sexual immorality and perversion. They serve as an example of those who suffer the punishment of eternal fire." Let us make our **church courts** so user friendly that no one has any excuse why they will not receive their inheritance, righteousness, peace, and joy in the Holy Spirit.

One day I was studying, and I got so excited about the faith message that I jumped up from the table and ran outside leaping and jumping for joy. During that revelation, the Holy Spirit said to me, "*Jesus is coming soon!*" It sobered me up! There is no time for anger, resentment, unresolved trivial disputes. Forgive and repent and be set free from the enemy. No doubt, Jesus is coming for a glorious, beautiful bride in the rapture of His church, a bride dressed in white linen (the good deeds of the saints), clothed in garments of salvation and royal robes of righteousness. Let us cleanse and purify our hearts now, *settle your trivial disputes*, be ready to come back and reign together with the Lord 1000 years when He comes to judge the world "and the angels who did not keep their positions of authority but abandoned their proper dwelling—" According to Matthew 11:28-30 AMP, "Come to me, all you who are weary and burdened, and I will give you rest. Take my yoke upon you and learn from me, for I am gentle and humble in heart, and you will find rest for your souls. For my yoke is easy and my burden is light."

Just do it! Follow your three-step trivial dispute resolution plan in chapter two. Let us give all the glory to Him who is able to keep you from stumbling and to present you before His glorious presence without fault and with great joy—to the only God our Savior be glory, majesty, power, and authority, through Jesus Christ our Lord, before all ages, now and forevermore! Amen. ***Come, Lord Jesus!***

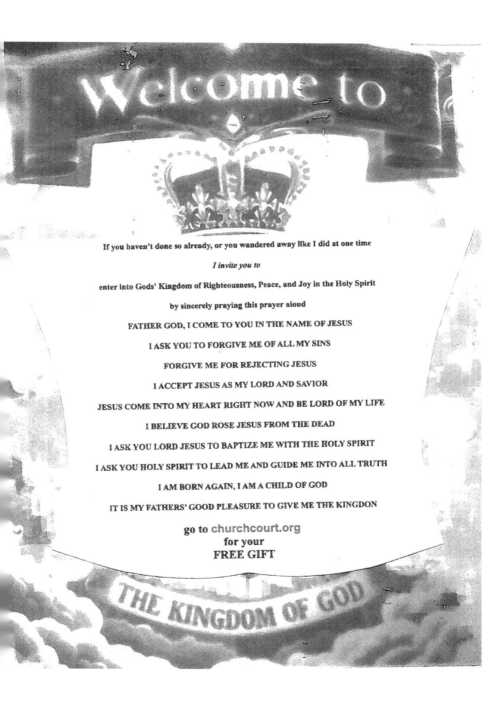

If you haven't done so already, or you wandered away like I did at one time

I invite you to

enter into Gods' Kingdom of Righteousness, Peace, and Joy in the Holy Spirit

by sincerely praying this prayer aloud

FATHER GOD, I COME TO YOU IN THE NAME OF JESUS

I ASK YOU TO FORGIVE ME OF ALL MY SINS

FORGIVE ME FOR REJECTING JESUS

I ACCEPT JESUS AS MY LORD AND SAVIOR

JESUS COME INTO MY HEART RIGHT NOW AND BE LORD OF MY LIFE

I BELIEVE GOD ROSE JESUS FROM THE DEAD

I ASK YOU LORD JESUS TO BAPTIZE ME WITH THE HOLY SPIRIT

I ASK YOU HOLY SPIRIT TO LEAD ME AND GUIDE ME INTO ALL TRUTH

I AM BORN AGAIN, I AM A CHILD OF GOD

IT IS MY FATHERS' GOOD PLEASURE TO GIVE ME THE KINGDON

go to **churchcourt.org**
for your
FREE GIFT

THE KINGDOM OF GOD

TO THE SHEEP

Jeremiah 3:15

"Then I will give you shepherds after my own heart, who will lead you with knowledge and understanding."

Ask God where your home church is.

TO THE SHEPHERDS

Acts 20:28 MSG

"Now it's up to you. Be on your toes—both for yourselves and your congregation of sheep. The Holy Spirit has put you in charge of these people—God's people they are—to guard and protect them. God himself thought they were worth dying for."

Glossary

Legal action: a dispute brought to a court of law for the purpose of seeking relief from or correcting an alleged wrong. Civil officers or overseers will administer the law that deals with offenses and hold hearings if necessary.

Civil matter: relating to citizens and their concerns.

Accuser: the person who starts a legal complaint against the one who harmed them in some way. (Plaintiff)

Respondent: the person who is accused of doing wrong and who should defend themselves. (Defendant)

Verified Complaint: a complaint that has been verified by the accuser that the facts stated in the complaint are true.

Invitation or summons: a form prepared by the accuser and issued by the official mediation parties that informs the respondent that they are invited to appear before the mediators to settle dispute. It may be served by an authorized person, such as a process server.

Answer: a respondent's written statement either to admit or deny the charges against them or demand more information about the claims of wrongdoing. The defendant may file an answer within 30 days of service of the complaint. An answer will be considered a request for an oral hearing with your

church court. The answer contains the defendant's response to the complaint.

Discovery: To begin preparing for your upcoming hearing, both sides engage in the formal process of exchanging information between the parties about the witnesses and evidence they will present at trial. Discovery enables the parties to know before the trial begins what evidence

may be presented.

Mediation: a process wherein the parties meet with a mutually selected impartial and neutral person/s who assists them in the negotiation of resolving their differences.

Forgive: a conscious, deliberate decision to release feelings of resentment or vengeance toward a

person or group who has harmed you, regardless of whether they deserve your forgiveness or not.

Repent: to be shown your faults scripturally and then to be shown how to scripturally correct the fault based on what the Word of God says is the right thing to do This will enable you to think in line with the thoughts of God so you can observe to do the right thing.

Meditate: think deeply or focus one's mind for a period of time, in silence or muttering aloud about what God has said to us. Turning over and around in the mind to gain greater understanding and be changed by God's truth.

CHURCH COURT

Go to

ChurchCourt.org

for

1. Church members pocket guide to trivial dispute resolution
2. An elder's pocket guide to set up your **church court**
3. "My Victory" dispute resolution journal
4. Church Court tv channels
5. Forms for filing your case in your church court
6. Contact information
7. Follow us on Facebook, Facebook Messenger, Instagram, YouTube
8. Church Court Institute

About the Author

Sharon Foster-Gautier is a licensed and ordained teacher of the Gospel of the Lord Jesus Christ. She believes that all scripture is given by the inspiration of God and is profitable for doctrine, for reproof, for correction, for instruction in righteousness, that the man/woman of God may be perfect, thoroughly equipped unto all good works" (2nd Timothy 3:16-17) She is married, has three grown children, nine grandchildren and two great-grandchildren so far. She enjoys family, cooking and gardening.

Go to ChurchCourt.org for contact information.

Printed in the USA
CPSIA information can be obtained
at www.ICGtesting.com
CBHW060747210724
11802CB00034B/684